Forestry

The Green World

Forestry

Catherine Raven

CHELSEA HOUSE
PUBLISHERS

An imprint of Infobase Publishing

Forestry

Copyright © 2006 by Infobase Publishing

Chelsea House
An imprint of Infobase Publishing
132 West 31st Street
New York NY 10001

Library of Congress Cataloging-in-Publication Data

Raven, Catherine, 1959–
   Forestry/Catherine Raven.
      p. cm. — (The Green World)
   ISBN 0-7910-8752-2
   1. Forests and forestry—Juvenile literature. 2. Forest ecology—Juvenile literature.
I. Title. II. Series.
SD376.R38 2005
634.9—dc22

                                                              2005021244

Chelsea House books are available at special discounts when purchased in bulk quantities for businesses, associations, institutions, or sales promotions. Please call our Special Sales Department in New York at (212) 967-8800 or (800) 322-8755.

You can find Chelsea House on the World Wide Web at http://www.chelseahouse.com

Text and cover design by Keith Trego

Printed in the United States of America

Bang 21C 10 9 8 7 6 5 4 3 2 1

This book is printed on acid-free paper.

All links, web addresses, and Internet search terms were checked and verified to be correct at the time of publication. Because of the dynamic nature of the web, some addresses and links may have changed since publication and may no longer be valid.

Table of Contents

Introduction

By William G. Hopkins

"Have you thanked a green plant today?" reads a popular bumper sticker. Indeed, we should thank green plants for providing the food we eat, fiber for the clothing we wear, wood for building our houses, and the oxygen we breathe. Without plants, humans and other animals simply could not exist. Psychologists tell us that plants also provide a sense of well-being and peace of mind, which is why we preserve forested parks in our cities, surround our homes with gardens, and install plants and flowers in our homes and workplaces. Gifts of flowers are the most popular way to acknowledge weddings, funerals, and other events of passage. Gardening is one of the fastest growing hobbies in North America and the production of ornamental plants contributes billions of dollars annually to the economy.

Human history has been strongly influenced by plants. The rise of agriculture in the Fertile Crescent of Mesopotamia brought previously scattered hunter-gatherers together into villages. Ever since, the availability of land and water for cultivating plants has been a major factor in determining the location of human settlements. World exploration and discovery was driven by the search for herbs and spices. The cultivation of New World crops—sugar, cotton, and tobacco—was responsible for the introduction of slavery to America, the human and social consequences of which are still with us. The push westward by English colonists into the rich lands of the Ohio River Valley in the mid-1700s was driven by the need to increase corn production and was a factor in precipitating the French and Indian War. The Irish Potato Famine in 1847 set in motion a wave of migration, mostly to North America, that would reduce the population of Ireland by half over the next 50 years.

As a young university instructor directing biology tutorials in a classroom that looked out over a wooded area, I would ask each group of students to look out the window and tell me what they saw. More often than not, the question would be met with a blank, questioning look. Plants are so much a part of our environment and the fabric of our everyday lives that they rarely register in our conscious thought. Yet today, faced with disappearing rainforests, exploding population growth, urban sprawl, and concerns about climate change, the productive capacity of global agricultural and forestry ecosystems is put under increasing pressure. Understanding plants is even more essential as we attempt to build a sustainable environment for the future.

THE GREEN WORLD series opens doors to the world of plants. The series describes what plants are, what plants do, and where plants fit into the overall circle of life. *Forestry* explores the science of forestry, from the types of trees and shrubs grown for commercial and medicinal use to the impact of trees on the environment and human society.

1 Welcome to the Forest Planet

Trees are your best antiques.
— Alexander Smith

Welcome to the Forest Planet

Space travel is no longer an oddity of science fiction. Photos of planets appear on our computer screens at the click of a button. These photos depict mountains and ridges, craters and cliffs, deserts, white clouds, active volcanoes, canyons, ancient hot springs, and oceans, all similar to Earth. Saturn has its rings; Mars is the red planet, and Neptune the blue. What is the distinguishing characteristic of Earth from other planets in the solar system? An astronaut might call us the Forest Planet. On the Forest Planet, North America is the guardian to over 15% of the world's forests. Forests are our great fortune and responsibility—they provide shelter and food for humans and wildlife. Left untouched, forests provide beauty and recreation that improves our quality of life. When removed, trees provide products that improve our lives, such as wood and paper. Who speaks for the many voices of people? Who speaks for the many voices of the forest? We have only one planet, so forestry science must speak for all.

THE FIRST FORESTERS

Forestry is the study of people and forests. People and forests have shared North America for over 30,000 years, but were unaware of each other until about 14,000 years ago. While pine and oak forests thrived in the southern part of the continent, people known as mammoth hunters lived in the far north, in the area between Canada's Mackenzie River and the coast of Alaska. Mammoth hunters lived on the **tundra,** where the frigid temperatures and permanently frozen soil, known as **permafrost,** prevented trees from growing. This was the last Ice Age, 30,000 years ago, and an enormous ice cap separated the northern people from the southern forests.

When the ice finally started to melt 15,000 years later, a relatively narrow ice-free corridor allowed the **Paleo-Indians** to move south. They moved rapidly, covering over 1,000 miles in 100 years. While people were moving south, the southern forests were migrating north. How do forests migrate? Seeds, which are actually baby trees wrapped up with some food, had lain long and patiently under the ice. As the ice retreated, the baby trees, mostly white spruce at the northern edge, burst out of the seed coat they had worn for thousands of years. In the wake of the retreating ice, **germinating** seeds slowly moved the forest north. In some melting areas, after the formation of soil, seeds blew in from nearby forests. Around 13,000 years ago, America's first explorers, the Paleo-Indians, bumped into the advancing forest. The exciting adventure of hunting mastodons, while giant short-faced bears and dire wolves hunted them, was ending. A new adventure was beginning. The Paleo-Indians were the first people in their lineage in over 30,000 years to see a forest.

At the same time that these Americans were beginning their difficult journey through the ice-free corridor, people in the Middle East ceased their nomadic lifestyle, settled down, and experimented with **agriculture**, the science of farming and raising crops, for the first time in human history. These two cultures, neither superior to the other, altered the relationship between humans and plants in important ways.

Archeological evidence shows that the first people began using and managing the forest resource right away. Their main tool was fire, which they used to clear the land, but they also selectively harvested wood and forest products. Paleo-Indians were woolly mammoth hunters, mastodon slayers, flint knappers, cave painters, and foresters.

WHAT IS FORESTRY?

Archeological evidence and oral history (history passed by word-of-mouth and not in books) provides information about prehistoric man's use of the forest. Paleo-Indians used the forests to cut logs for their houses and canoes, hunted forest animals for food, and ate pine nuts and acorns from forest trees. Wood fuel replaced the mammoth dung (manure) that had kept their campfires burning on the long trek to the warmer land. In the western part of the continent, redwood bark was stripped into long thin strands that provided most of the fibers necessary for clothing and baskets. The forest also provided a source for stories, religion, and art.

Imagine a tribal meeting several thousand years ago in the Pacific Coast forest to discuss wild ginger (*Asarum*). Growing only in the dark, damp, interior of very old forests, ginger is a source of medicine and food. Wild ginger has wide, velvety, heart-shaped leaves, and three long maroon tubular petals that form the plant's single flower. It is the root that harvesters seek, and taking it kills the plant. Although not related to the ginger (*Zingiber officinale*) used to flavor pumpkin pies, the taste is nearly identical. At the camp-fire, one man speaks in favor of banning all ginger digging, because deer and rabbits, both important sources of food, eat the leaves. Another man speaks about the sacred nature of the plant. He is concerned that cutting trees, even the maple saplings, kills the ginger on the forest floor. He wants to stop all maple cutting. Still another speaks for more fires, which will probably kill the ginger. "Winter is coming," he says, "we must burn to increase the huckleberry crop." When an argument starts, he replies, "We have been without ginger before." Still another asks to stop the burning, and harvest all the roots they can find. "The ginger root is easy to dry and carry," he says, "We need it for trade with the other tribes." Some people don't like the idea of using or killing everything, while others are ready to pick up and move when they deplete the resources. Today, foresters refer to these various people as **stakeholders**, citizens with an interest in the use of the forest. They are a necessary part of forest management.

One woman knows more than anyone about plants. She has learned from her ancestors and from experimentation, and she will take charge of the ginger issue. She needs to know more than human values to manage the forest; she needs to understand nature. Understanding begins with the **scientific method**. She will follow the route that humans have always used to learn about the natural world. The process begins with observations. It will take many years, but her observations will lead her to find the following pattern: berries are few in the presence of ginger. Following the observations, there will be a question. Does the root medicine in the ginger prohibit the berries from growing? Her answer will come from testing. She will plant the ginger next to berries, see if the shrubs die, and use the results to guide her actions and suggest further questions. She has a simple explanation for what is going on; perhaps she is right, perhaps not. We call this tentative explanation a **hypothesis**. It is only one very small step. She learned about nature and listened to the people. In this manner of learning and listening, she became a forester.

WHAT IS A FOREST?

A forest is a naturally occurring biological **community** dominated by trees (Figure 1.1). Biologists define *community* as a group of interacting species. In natural forest communities, man has not planted the trees, and all the life stages of the trees are present: seeds, seedlings, mature trees, injured trees, infected trees, dead standing trees, and dead and down trees. How do we know if trees dominate a community? Trees live in many communities that they do not dominate: parklands, wetlands, shrublands, and woodlands. Although most people can recognize a forest, foresters often rely on a variety of objective means to distinguish a tree-dominated community. Sometimes a strict definition is important. For example, if I tell you forests cover 28% of Montana, you will want to know how I defined *forest*. Most scientists use **canopy** measurements to define a forest. The canopy is the roof of the forest created by boughs and branches from one tree interweaving with neighboring trees. Take a stroll through a forest with your friends, stopping several times to look straight up. Is there open sky or part of a tree over your head? Scientists ask that question, and carefully calculate the percent of a forest or wooded area that has a canopy. Generally, a forest has 40% canopy cover.

Figure 1.1 The presence of trees alone is not enough to make a forest. A forest is a naturally occurring community, encompassing many species of plants, animals, fungi, and bacteria. Trees are the most influential members of the forest community.

A forest is not a tree farm. A tree farm uses mechanically assisted planting. The trees don't just grow where the seeds land, they are planted by machine, or human hand, and on some occasions seeds are sprayed from fixed-wing aircraft. Owners rarely allow trees to become old before harvesting. Trees on a tree farm almost never die a natural death. In addition, there will be very few animals, bugs, and fungus, even though they are natural and native, because they eat trees and are not welcome on a tree farm. Therefore, tree farms must employ synthetic (non-natural) pesticides and insecticides. Large-scale tree farms are often called plantations.

WHAT ARE THE DIFFERENT TYPES OF FOREST?

One way to characterize a forest is whether it has a closed or open canopy. If at least 70% of the area is covered, then the forest is "closed canopy." Open canopy forests are those with a roof covering 40% to 70% of the total area. Tropical rainforests, because they are so dense with trees, often have 100% canopy closure.

Why Aren't There Forests in the Great Plains?

The Great Lost Spruce Forest is an appropriate name for the land we know today as the Great Plains. During the last ice age, white spruce (*Picea glauca*), blue spruce (*Picea pungens*), and some limber pine (*Pinus flexilis*) dominated the ancient forest in the ice-free region between the Rockies and the Atlantic coast. Shade intolerant **forbs** (non-woody, non-grass-like plants) grew on the forest floor and received plenty of sunlight through the widely spaced trees. Prairie grasslands interspersed with the trees. When the climate began to warm, the spruce forest failed in the heat and drought. Today, the meager precipitation that falls in the Plains evaporates quickly in the wind and sun. Yet, areas in the Rocky Mountains with just as little precipitation support trees. This is because roots in the Rockies region can draw water from the ancient underground glacial lakes or aquifers, a resource lacking in the Great Plains. The heat and drought increased the occurrence of wildfires to which spruce trees, with their beautiful, long, ground-sweeping skirts, would be especially susceptible. Limber pines reestablish slowly following a fire because they produce very few seed cones and none at all until they are relatively old. Trees that shed or lack lower branches and are very prolific, such as the lodgepole pine (*Pinus contorta*), are more fire resistant.

Prairie grasses filled in the spaces left by the drying and burning spruce and pine trees, successfully colonizing nearly the entire area about 8,000 years ago. Scientists today are asking whether forests will re-enter the Plains. A 2003 study completed by the National Academy of Sciences predicts a decrease in precipitation along with a 10.5°F (5.84°C) increase in average temperature in the Great Plains by the end of this century. Will forests return?

We also divide forests into two broad classes depending upon whether the dominant trees are **gymnosperms** or **angiosperms.** You might be familiar with the synonymous terms **hardwood**, the wood of an angiosperm, and **softwood**, the wood of a gymnosperm. These common terms no longer characterize the relative durability of the wood (see Chapter 4), but you should be familiar with them nonetheless. In the forests of North America, gymnosperms are evergreen, cone-bearing trees with needle-type leaves. The only two exceptions are larch (also known as tamarack), which is not evergreen and yew, which is not cone-bearing. Common gymnosperms with straight needles are pine, fir, and spruce. Cedar, juniper, and cypress have small cupped or curved needles that may look like scales. Originating 300 million years ago, these are among the very first trees ever to appear on planet Earth. They dominated the forests during the age of dinosaurs; look for them the next time you watch the movie "Jurassic Park."

Angiosperm trees are easily recognized by their broad leaves. A broadleaf is wide and flat like a maple, oak, or poplar. Most angiosperm trees are **deciduous**, shedding in the fall—a sharp contrast to the evergreen gymnosperms. Angiosperms first appeared on Earth only about 120 million years ago. They invaded the **conifer** forests at the time when mammals were chasing the dinosaurs into extinction. Separated in the fossil record by hundreds of millions of years, today we find hardwoods and softwoods fully integrated and living side-by-side in only two of the eight common forest regions of North America.

North America's forests (Figure 1.2) stretch from east to west across the northern part of the continent and the length of both coasts, like a wide, inverted "U." The southernmost tip of the continent, the tail curling northeast toward Florida, is home of our tropical forest, as is the tip of Florida. The Great Plains, the western desert between the Pacific Coast and the Rockies, and the far northern permafrost belt are the three large areas lacking forests. Foresters split the continent into eight regions.

Figure 1.2 In North America, you can trace a belt of forests from the southeast corner of Florida north to the Canadian arctic, then west to the Pacific coast, and south along the entire coast.

Gymnosperms dominate four: Pacific Coast, boreal forest, Rocky Mountain, and southern conifer. Angiosperms dominate the central mixed, northern hardwoods, tropical rainforest, and bottomlands hardwood. The northernmost forest, stretching across Canada from east to west, is the **boreal** forest, also known as the northern coniferous forest or **taiga**. Spruce dominated, with a lush green carpet, it most closely resembles the very first American forests seen by man. Due to the cold temperatures and indirect sunlight, there is very little evaporation here. The taiga is a relatively wet forest dotted with lakes, bogs, and **fens**. This forest survives at the border of the treeless tundra, in the coldest region of any of our forests, and is home to caribou, lynx, moose, wood bison, wolves, and the great grey owl.

South of the taiga, there are two forest regions west of the Great Plains and four to the east. One of the western forests runs along the Pacific Coast and the other along the Rocky Mountains. The Pacific Coast forest, stretching from Alaska through Canada to Baja California, including the Cascade and Sierra Ranges, is home of the world famous coastal redwoods (Sequoia sempervirens) and giant sequoias (Sequoia giganteum). If a tree could travel, this is where it would go. All the trees are bigger, taller, and older than in any other region in which they grow. Some of the trees here are thousands of years old. The Rocky Mountain forest region consists of a very patchy group of forests rather than a continuous interconnected band. The main reason for the patchiness is the strong south aspect effect: slopes facing south are generally too dry to support forests. Subalpine fir, spruce, and whitebark pine grow at highest elevations with ponderosa pine and Douglas fir thriving in the lower, drier sites. These forests, far removed from dense human cities, support a large number of wildlife species. Most of the country's **virgin forests** are here. "Virgin" designates a forest that has escaped logging or intentional burning.

East of the Plains, three forest regions are oriented along a north–south gradient. Farthest north, the northern hardwoods forest of beech, birch, and maple crosses the U.S.-Canadian boundary. The oak dominated central mixed forest, heavily logged, contains few virgin stands. The region is home to the densest human population in the United States. Heat tolerant, long-needled loblolly pine characterizes the southern pine forest in the southeastern United States. The forest floor is dry, brown, and sparse. As with the central mixed, the timber industry has replaced virtually all of the virgin stands with tree farms. Along the Mississippi Valley delta and along the Gulf of Mexico, the bottomlands hardwoods region intrudes into the southern pine region. The region includes swamps and cypress groves, in addition to typical hardwoods: maple, dogwood, and hickory.

Tropical rainforests grow along the southern curl of the continent in Mexico, and into Florida, where they are mostly contained within Everglades National Park. Rainfall from 79 to 158 inches per year, no dry season, and evergreen broadleaf trees characterize the rainforest. Precipitation and elevation generally determine the makeup of the several classes of rainforests in Mexico. Among the dozens of tree species are oak, pine, mangrove, and acacia.

Connections

Forestry, first practiced in North America 13,000 years ago by Paleo-Indians, is the art and science of managing forests. Science flows like a river, generally in one direction toward a final goal. Culture is a crooked creek, and sometimes turns back on itself, leaving followers stranded in the oxbow. We will generally follow the course of science and allow you to make your own value judgments as we proceed.

A forest is a biological community dominated by trees. We will discuss, compare, and contrast the distinct types of trees that are important in North America's forests in the following two chapters. We will begin with the ancient coniferous forests and proceed to the younger hardwoods, including the broad-leaves of the rainforest. Next, we will put the trees back in the forest and examine the house that we have created, the forest ecosystem, from top to bottom, canopy to ground cover. Once we understand the forests, we will examine forest **ecology**, the study of how the forest interacts with the world around it. For our capstone chapter, we will apply everything we have learned to look at forest fire ecology and the practice of forest management.

2 Tree Talk:
The Physiology of How Trees Grow

In some mysterious way woods have never seemed to me to be static things. In physical terms, I move through them; yet in metaphysical ones, they seem to move through me.
— John Fowles

Tree Talk:
The Physiology of How Trees Grow

Did you know trees could talk? On your next visit to a forest, *look*, don't listen, for talking trees. Indians often used trees to talk to each other. They bent the tops of hardwood saplings to the ground so they could root from the tops and form gentle arches that say "Here! Over here! This way!" Trappers and mountain men cut blazes into trees. A blaze is a carved area on a tree trunk that provides trail information. The boundary markers that settlers carved into trees when they came west in the late 1800s are still visible today. The tree with one spot nicked either by Indian, mountain man, or early surveyor says, "Welcome. Your trail begins here." The one with the three slashes shouts, "Stop! Warning!" These marks are what Ernest Thompson Seton, founder of the Boy Scouts of America, calls the "universal language of the woods." *How can trees continue to grow for hundreds of years and still bear these original messages? Why don't the blazes disappear as the trees grow taller? Why doesn't the tree bark grow around these marks? Do blazes kill trees?* In this chapter we'll discuss the means by which forest trees grow, age, and reproduce, so next time a tree gives a signal, you won't be surprised that it has been talking for hundreds of years.

A TREE IS BORN

All trees have a similar **life cycle**, a means of growing, reproducing, and aging. A tree begins life inside a **seed**. Inside the seed are the three main parts of a tree: stem, leaf, and root. All the parts of the full-grown tree belong to one of these three groups. The leaves inside the seeds are called **cotyledons**. Gymnosperms may have several cotyledons, but will usually have eight. Angiosperms have either one or two cotyledons, but angiosperm *trees* always have two, and are therefore called **dicotyledons** (*di* means two in Greek) or dicots, for short. A protective casing, the seed coat covers the tiny tree. The tree inside the seed cannot absorb the sun's rays and provide its own energy needs like other plants, so when the mother tree makes the seed she is always sure to include some food. The baby tree needs enough food to survive until it breaks through the seed coat and unfurls its tiny leaves toward the sun. Trees that don't exit their seed right away may remain dormant, alive but essentially sleeping, in the soil. If we think of the food in the seed as "freeze-dried," it is easy to see that the basic requirement for breaking **dormancy** is *warm* water to transform the freeze-dried food into useable energy for the tree. Beyond this general need, there are various species-specific requirements for breaking dormancy; some seeds even need to pass through the digestive tract of an animal before the little seed trees can emerge. Animal digestive systems contain chemicals that break down the seed coat.

Dormant seeds in soil are part of the **soil seed bank**—the seeds held in reserve by the forest until the time is right for germination. **Germination** is the process by which the trees grow through the seed and pop open their coat. How many tree seeds are in the soil bank? Trees dominate a forest because of their size and height, but the number of trees is almost always less than the number of **forbs** (non-woody plants that are not grasses) or grasses. Therefore, compared to weeds and other colonizing plants, forest trees have relatively small seed bank deposits. Although comparatively small, they are long-lived. Though tree seeds will generally only survive dormancy for a few decades, some evergreen seeds may persist in the soil for hundreds of years. One angiosperm tree, a palm, germinated following a 2,000-year dormancy.

The greatest difference between angiosperm and gymnosperm trees is the presentation and growth of the seed. The evergreen seed (*sperma* in Greek) grows bare and alone from the fertilized cell. As opposed to the naked seed of the gymnosperm (*gymnos* in Greek), the dicot seed is born and grows within an *angion* or vessel. The vessel, also known as the **carpel**, is a part of the flower. Unlike the naked seeded evergreens, angiosperm seeds have a cozy carpel to cradle and protect them.

Not all trees begin life as a seed. Some trees begin life by way of asexual reproduction. Asexual reproduction occurs in the absence of pollen and egg; the new tree simply sprouts off part of the parent. Asexual reproduction yields new trees that are genetic clones of the parent tree. Although these clones look like independent trees, and we call them trees, they are attached under the soil and out of sight, to the parent tree's body; these clones are apendages, and not independent trees at all. Sexually reproduced seeds, those produced when pollen fertilizes an egg, will become genetically unique trees. Most trees only produce asexually when the environment is too harsh to allow for the energetically rigorous demands of producing pollen, egg, flower, and seed. High-elevation trees often reproduce without seeds, but it is a rarity among *forest* trees. Any environment too unfriendly to allow sexual reproduction is probably too harsh for a forest to thrive. Exceptions are redwoods, short leaf and pitch pine, and aspen.

THE TREE GROWS

Trees and daisies are both the same size when their life begins. The daisy may die within a year and reach heights of about 3 feet (1 meter), while the tree may live for thousands of years and grow to 300 feet (100 meters) tall. Hold two seeds in your hand, a daisy and a sequoia. One has the potential to reach several tons and live for thousands of years while the other will probably die a year later after producing less than a pound of living tissue.

A tree grows by increasing its length and its girth. Elongation allows trees to grow up, down, and out with shoots and branches that are taller, deeper, and longer. This type of growth, called **primary growth**, does not produce bark. Trees elongate from **apical meristem**, generative (growth capable) tissue located at the tips of the roots, the topmost stem, and the branches. The apical meristem at the topmost stem is located within the **apical buds**, and at the sides of the stem it is located in **lateral buds.** The tree expects to open the apical buds annually. Lateral buds, unlike apical buds, do not usually open annually because the apical buds send them chemical messages telling them not to open. Lateral buds may stay closed indefinitely, remaining in place alongside the tree trunk for decades until disease, browsing, or environmental stress removes the influence of the apical bud and allows the telescoped stem within to burst forth into a new side branch. **Browsing** describes the activity of animals feeding upon woody plants such as trees and shrubs. Browsing is analogous to grazing, the act of animals feeding on non-woody plants such as grasses and forbs.

Primary growth occurs through cell division. One cell divides into two and each daughter cell then becomes as large as the parent cell. Daughter cells each divide into two and grow again. All plants, including the gigantic tree and the little daisy, grow from apical meristems. The herbaceous plant will complete all its needs—shoots, roots, and leaves—using primary growth.

Shoot growth pattern determines the general shape of the tree and is guided by genes and environment. Trees that grow higher faster than they grow wider will be tall and conical like pine and firs. This branching pattern is called **excurrent**. The reverse pattern, **decurrent**, is a rounder shape like the classic oaks. Evergreen trees tend to grow from one main stem, while broadleaved trees tend to ramble, look more rounded, and often don't have an obvious main stem. Environmental conditions may affect growth patterns. If an animal eats the apical bud, the lateral buds may grow out and make the tree wider. Strong winds may also permanently deform the shape of a tree so that it resembles a flag with all the branches on the leeward side (the side opposite from where the wind is coming from). High altitude may cause trees to grow stunted and in a circular patch (see "Krumholtz" box).

The power of the tree to become huge lies not with the primary but with the **secondary growth**, a physiological adaptation unique to woody plants. The tree's main shoot, branches, and roots all increase their diameter as the tree ages. Secondary growth derives from the **cambium**, which is a **lateral meristem**, as opposed to the apical (top) meristem of primary growth. Cambium lies between the inner bark and the wood. When the meristem cell divides into two cells, one will become wood, and one bark. The cambium layer is thus responsible for production of both wood and bark along the entire main branch of the tree, all lateral branches, and the roots. We don't usually think about roots as having bark, but all tree roots that are not fine, temporary hairs, will gain girth by way of the cambium layer. The outermost bark cannot keep up with the expanding girth of the wood so it dies and sloughs as new bark takes its place.

Lying between the inner bark and the wood, the cambium is protected by the outer bark. When animals or humans cut into and through the entire outer bark, they are most certainly reaching and damaging the cambium. Cambium is not replaceable. When buffalo or trappers blazed a tree, they removed both the bark and the cambium, thus preventing their mark from ever again increasing in girth. The tree around the blaze will continue to grow outwards, thus giving the scar or blaze a recessed appearance.

MORE TREE TALK: ANNUAL RINGS

The cells produced by the cambium are large and loosely compacted early in the growing season. Later, they become tiny, tightly packed, and thus a higher density. When the next growing season begins the newer larger cells lay adjacent to the past year's tightly packed tiny cells. This dramatic difference is visible to the eye and allows the tree to tell us how old it is: we simply count the **annual rings**, the lines of densely packed cells (Figure 2.1). Of course, trees growing in a tropical climate won't have easily distinguishable rings because there is no early and late growing season—trees grow nearly continuously in the tropics. Annual rings are clear enough to remain visible even on petrified wood that is millions of years old.

Figure 2.1 This transverse section slice of a cold climate tree has dark bands where late season cambium cells are tightly compacted.

FUELING THE GROWTH: PHOTOSYNTHESIS AND WATER

Trees need a lot of energy to fuel their explosive and sustained growth. Plants meet their energy needs through photosynthesis, the production of carbohydrates in the presence of carbon dioxide and water. Carbohydrates are the building block of plants and food for humans. Capturing the sun's energy is the job of the leaves. Evergreen trees, which have needle shaped leaves that are less adept at absorption, can produce as much net annual energy as a broadleaved trees because they work year-round. Broadleaves can capture a significantly larger amount of light, but are only seasonally active. Broadleaves fall off and leave the tree in semi-slumber during the winter season.

Water, besides being the source for the oxygen produced during photosynthesis, is also necessary to provide cell shape. Water takes up most of the space in the tree cells and therefore provides the rigidity and plumpness that gives the cells their structure.

Krumholtz

We know that forests cannot exist in the absence of water, or in the extremes of the polar regions. These environments simply cannot meet the physiological requirements of trees. But not all trees are alike. There are always a few trees that venture beyond the places to which life tries to restrict them.

The wintry extent of the forest, the places that are too cold and too windy for almost all trees, is the indefinite zone we call the subalpine. While one edge of the subalpine borders the forest, the other edge borders the tree line. Tree line is the imaginary and usually undulating line beyond which trees cannot grow due to cold and wind. Inhabiting this fringe area are krumholtz formation trees. These are the renegades that are whipped by the weather until the only remaining branches are on the leeward side. These scrawny posts resemble not so much trees as flags.

Krumholtz, from the German word meaning "crooked wood," is more common to some species than others. Mountain hemlock (*Tsuga mertensiana*), alpine fir (*Abies lasiocarpa*), bristlecone pine (*Pinus aristata*), whitebark pine (*Pinus albicaulis*), and limber pine (*Pinus flexilis*) bend willingly to the north winds, forming crooked and knotted stems. Growing horizontally more than vertically, they scarcely resemble their forest siblings. Don't look for pinecones; most krumholtz formation trees are obliged to reproduce vegetatively.

You can see krumholtz formation in areas where forests yield to the northern latitudes or high altitude. The elevation of the tree line varies with latitude; as you travel north, the elevation of the timberline lowers. In the northern Rockies, at the 45th parallel, forests thrive above 8,000 feet (2,450 meters). Head straight north to the 49th parallel, and you'll find "flag trees"

This plumpness, caused by the inner pressure of the water against the cell walls is called turgor, and maintains the upright posture of the plant. Water comes to the plant from the soil, by way of the root hairs and the roots, then travels through the

Two hoary marmots in heated discussion in front of a subalpine cluster of fir. One fir, barely wider than the rodent, has grown taller than a shrub, but reproduces vegetatively. Forming a tight circle around the parent tree, the offspring, hundreds of years old, are only a bit taller than the marmots.

waving their surrender to the environment at 6,400 feet (1,950 meters). In Fernie, British Columbia, the tree line is only 6,000 feet (1,830 meters).

Keep an eye on these fascinating zones for this is the area where global climate change will have the most noticeable effect. Here in the fuzzy boundaries, the forests will either recede to where even the krumholtz disappears or grow right into and pass the tree line. Most likely you will be able to witness both in your lifetime if you get to know the subalpine zones.

entire plant along vessels, and exits the tree through **transpiration** at the leaves. Broadleaved plants transpire more than needle-leaved plants. Environmental conditions affect transpiration as well. Heat increases transpiration. The number of pores, called **stoma**, in the leaves and shoots also affects transpiration. Trees can react to changing water conditions by closing and opening their stoma. In the case of severe water shortage, stoma regulation may be insufficient. In that case, trees sacrifice their root hairs and leaves and in severe shortages, trees may die.

COMPLETING THE CYCLE: REPRODUCTION AND SENESCENCE

Trees begin to reproduce at various ages depending upon the species and the environment. Between the ages of five and 20, trees mature and become capable of sexual reproduction. In the Northern Rockies, lodgepole pine reproduce by age eight, and in the cold boreal forest, a white pine may be nearly 30 before maturing. Gymnosperms and angiosperms each have a unique means of reproduction, but both utilize pollen and ovules (eggs). The softwood ovules lay within the structures commonly called "pinecones." Pinecones are actually **megasporangia** or ovulate cones (Figure 2.2). The pollen is contained in the **microsporangia**, which are soft, small, fragile, and inconspicuous cones only about an inch (less than 3 centimeters) long. Both male and female cones grow on the same tree, but the pollen cones tend to be lower, which decreases the possibility of self-pollination (an egg and pollen coming from the same tree or inbreeding, which may make offspring less able to survive). When wind-blown pollen fertilizes the ovule, the embryonic tree begins to develop. The entire seed is produced within the ovulate cone. In order to continue their life cycle, the seeds must leave the cone. Some cones drop from the branches, shattering and releasing the seeds directly to the ground. Some seeds, especially the larger seeds of the limber and white pines, are eaten right out of the cones by birds and other wildlife and redistributed in the animal's

Figure 2.2 To produce a tree embryo, seen here in its seed coat (A), requires pollen from the microsporangia or pinecone (B) to fertilize the egg cell within the megasporangia (C).

droppings to begin life far away from the parent tree. Wind often displaces the light, winged seeds.

Angiosperms, which are flowering plants, produce their reproductive structures from apical meristems like the gymnosperms, but do not always bear pollen and ovules on the same tree. As with the conifers, wind may sweep the pollen to eggs. Animals also disperse hardwood pollen inadvertently; birds, bats, bees, and other insects often seek the tasty rewards of the flower. Unlike the bare, exposed seeds of the gymnosperm trees, angiosperms encase their seeds in **fruit**, a specialized and more modern adaptation than the naked seed.

Mature trees eventually age. Although most trees die of external causes such as disease or human damage, those that live long enough will die of old age. The first sign of aging in a tree is a reduced rate of growth. Reduced growth rates may be manifest by a lessening ability to carry water to the appendages that are furthest from the soil (the water source). These appendages then begin to die off, creating the familiar "bald" top tree, one with a dead crown.

Connections

Trees talk. They talk to themselves and they talk to us. Apical buds send messages to lateral buds to keep them from growing. Lateral buds respond, "I'm coming out now!" when they've been browsed. Blazes carved into trees by buffalo are commonly found in Yellowstone National Park, and may be hundreds of years old. Animals only mark part of the tree and not all the way around the circumference, so the cambium layer remains active and continues to produce bark, increasing the girth of the tree everywhere except at the blaze. Eventually the blaze becomes recessed and we can get an idea of how long ago the trail was buffalo blazed by measuring the distance from the blaze to the outermost bark (Figure 2.3).

Figure 2.3 The lodgepole pines in the foreground are marked with buffalo blazes. Perhaps 100 years old, the blazes still speak to the bull in the distant meadow.

All trees have a similar life cycle, beginning in a seed, waiting until conditions are ripe for germination, and then living for various years as an immature or young tree. Eventually they develop reproductive structures: flowers in the case of angiosperms, and cones in the case of gymnosperms. When they are able to reproduce, they are considered mature trees. Mature trees eventually get old, grow slower, succumb to disease, or simply die of old age by outgrowing the ability of their body to transport the necessary water and nutrients.

In the following two chapters, we'll concentrate on the special growth patterns of the two major classes of forest trees: gymnosperms in Chapter 3 and angiosperms in Chapter 4.

3 The Kings:
Forest Gymnosperms

*It may be that some time an immortal pine will be
the flag of a united and peaceful world.*

— Enos A. Mills

The Kings:
Forest Gymnosperms

In the Wyoming Yellowstone River Valley, a redwood tree with a four-foot diameter rises out of a hillside at 8,200 feet (2,500 meters) elevation. As the rains continue to wash away the surrounding soil, more trees are revealed. All of the trees are snags, which are main trunks without branches. You hike for half an hour up the hill to the trees for a close inspection and find an exposed snag with annual growth rings almost a quarter of an inch wide.

This is odd, because with so little rain falling here, growth rings tend to be narrow. The growing season here is only about five weeks and on the dry slopes there is very little moisture, producing annual growth among evergreens of about one-sixteenth inch. Further confusing the picture is the fact that redwoods don't grow in Wyoming. But they grew here 50 million years ago, when a volcanic eruption covered them with ash as they stood watch over horse, rhinoceros, and camels grazing on the subtropical floodplain below. At the time of the eruptions, gymnosperms, having spent hundreds of millions of years adapting to the environment, were at the apex of their planetary dominance. While the trees from one forest were turning to stone, soil was forming upon where another forest grew. Flowering trees were new to the planet then and just beginning to wage war for resources with the established giants. Before the volcanoes became dormant, as many as 50 different forests, separated by about a million years each, grew and became petrified here (Figure 3.1). How have these massive trees been able to survive and dominate so many forest ecosystems for so long, even with the young angiosperms nipping at their heels? Will the gymnosperms remain forest kings into the next millennia or are these giants just relics doomed to yield the forest to the invading angiosperms?

CONIFER VS. BROADLEAF FORESTS

In this chapter, we meet the forest giants, gymnosperms, living in a world in which they are not entirely comfortable. After all, they are the trees of the long past Ice Age. One potential

Figure 3.1 Above the Slough Creek in northwest Wyoming, an ancient gymnosperm, turned to stone as many as 50 million years ago, stands sentinel next to a live Douglas fir.

problem is their vigorous competitor, the angiosperms. Another problem is a climate that is becoming warmer and drier. In the previous chapter, we discussed some basic differences between gymnosperms and angiosperms. Recall that the conifers dominate the coldest forested regions of the world, the taiga, or the boreal forest. Conifers tend to be bigger, older, and taller than broadleaved trees. They favor diffuse roots over taproots. They are better able to withstand water shortages and strong winds. In this chapter, we'll identify the major coniferous trees of the forest and discuss their adaptations. We will closely examine eight groups of **Coniferophyta** (coniferous plants) that are common in North America.

There are three families of forest Coniferophyta (Latin name in parentheses follows the common name): pine (Pinaceae), taxodium (Taxodiaceae), and cypress (Cupressaceae). Pinaceae are further subdivided into six smaller groups called genera (the singular of genera is genus):

1. hemlock (*Tsuga*)

2. Douglas fir (*Pseudotsuga*)

3. larch (*Larix*)

4. spruce (*Picea*)

5. fir (*Abies*)

6. pines (*Pinus*)

Note that the genus name, by convention, follows in parenthesis and is italicized. Pine is both a family name and a genus name, so we will use the formal term Pinaceae when referring to the pine family. Taxodium and cypress each possess one common evergreen forest tree, the redwood and cedar, respectively. Giant sequoia, an uncommon forest tree found only in scattered groves along the west side of the Sierras, is also a member of the Taxodium family. Although each genus is further divided into species, we will concentrate on genus and family level characteristics. First, let's consider the entire group of gymnosperms.

Most gymnosperms rely on wind to disperse their seeds, and a few are dispersed by animals. In order to facilitate wind dispersal, most of the common forest evergreens have winged seeds. Although the seeds vary in size, most are tiny—too small to provide a meal for an animal. The seeds that are wingless are also big and tasty and can entice hungry animals to transport them. Why not just plop right down below the tree? Many evergreens are not shade tolerant, so their seeds must seek territory beyond the shade of their mother's canopy. The seedlings must be planted beyond the skirt, not the canopy, in order to receive sufficient sunlight. The seeds that are wingless are also big and tasty and can thus entice hungry animals to transport them.

Coniferophyta are not as variable as the flowering trees. Strongly excurrent, most have a classic conical shape. There are only three leaf patterns among forest conifers: single needle attachment, multiple needle attachment, and scale-like needles. Scale-like needles appear only on redwoods and red cedar. With the exception of larch, all gymnosperms are evergreens. All but the pines have short needles, rarely much more than about 1 inch (3 centimeters) long. All gymnosperm *forest* trees are **monoecious**, meaning that both pollen-bearing cones and seed-producing cones grow on the same tree.

One thing that distinguishes forest trees from those growing in grasslands or parklands is that forest trees are willing to share resources with other trees. However, they have preferences, and each genus prefers certain neighbors to others. Spruce and larch share well together in the northern coniferous forest because spruce readily yields the wettest sites to the larch. Along the Pacific Coast, shade tolerant hemlock grows well with Douglas fir, cedar, and redwoods. The northernmost Pacific Coast is home to mixed hemlock and spruce forests. At high elevations throughout evergreen forest country, spruce shares the short growing season with subalpine fir. Gymnosperms that don't share well, when found growing together, are usually fighting over resources: whitebark pine, lodgepole, and subalpine fir, for example.

SPRUCE

We will first consider spruce, which you recall was the main component of the Ice Age forests. The spruce is recognized by its sharp, single needles. All other single-needle Pinaceae are soft, not sharp. Spruce still dominates the coldest and largest forest on the continent, the boreal. Also common in the northern hardwoods zone, spruce try more than any other evergreen to keep their feet wet, and they often manage by living within damp forest seeps or swamps. With a low, full sweeping skirt of branches and a very thin, flaky bark, spruce are not well adapted to survive fire. Still, you should not be surprised if after a fire you find the charred soil covered with spruce seeds. The adult trees may all be dead because the fire encircled their entire lower cambium, however, the cones which sit near the top of the tree, remained safely above the flames.

The presence of spruce in a forest is largely dependent upon surface water availability. When the forest becomes water stressed, the spruce dies back and pines increase. When the rains return and the pines start to waterlog, the spruce grow back.

Spruce is renown for its bluish color, which is the result of a wax coating on its needles. Commercial breeders often select for the blue color, but even in the wild, all spruce is bluer than other Pinaceae. Two well-known varieties of spruce are Sitka and Engelmann. Sitka spruce is specialized for salt-spray and is able to extend the forest along the windy Pacific Coast in areas impossible for other trees to survive. Engelmann spruce can survive at the highest forested mountain elevations, living along with subalpine fir at the edge of the alpine zone.

FIR

Firs are common in all but the warmest and driest evergreen forests. They are well adapted to cold and snow. They have a classic conical shape, short soft single needles, and are distinguished by having erect cones that point straight up from the branches, as opposed to the other single-needled trees whose cones hang down. The cones are very fragile, breaking apart as soon as they hit the ground. Fir bark, which is thin and covered with highly flammable pitch blisters, ignites easily. Among the earliest English-speaking visitors west of the Great Plains, Meriwether Lewis and William Clark reported in their journals of 1803–1805 of having watched Indians turn trees into giant torches during celebrations. Although they didn't mention the genus, the trees the Indians were torching almost certainly were fir.

Firs fight with pines and Douglas firs for resources (Figure 3.2). When the altitude increases and the weather gets tough, the firs have an advantage. When the climate starts to desiccate and fires are frequent, you'll want to put your money on the pine. One well-known fir is subalpine, easily recognized by the pointy witch's cap top.

Douglas fir (aka Doug) is not actually a fir nor is it in the genus Abies. The scientific name, *Pseudotsuga*, means false hemlock. Not only is it *not* a fir, it is also *not* a hemlock. Once thought to be a pine, then a fir, then a hemlock, it finally was recognized in a genus all its own. Dougs grow all over the world, and all species in this genus are genetically very similar. Dougs are well adapted to a hot, dry **habitat** that burns regularly. Their roots can grow straight down relatively rapidly to absorb deep underground water when surface water is scarce. The bark is very thick and corky, providing maximum fire resistance, and the branches do not droop to the ground on mature trees, thus staying away from the flame of ground fires. Their generally upturned branches are a detriment in snowy country because they don't shed snow as rapidly as the hemlocks, spruces, and witch cap firs. Dougs are recognized by unique cones that appear to have little mouse tails coming out of the bracts.

Figure 3.2 A pine tree, a Douglas fir (which is not a fir tree), and a fir grow side-by-side near the subalpine zone fighting for resources. A large tree in the middle is the Doug. To its right, and also on the far left are pine trees. The tallest tree, on the Doug's left, is a subalpine fir. Note the upturned branches of the pine are opposite of the downward sloping branches of the fir. Also compare the narrow pointy cap on the fir with the broad rounded top of the Doug and the classic evergreen shaped pine. The Doug is adapted to drought, the fir to heavy snow, and the pine to fire. Can you see how environmental disturbances will shift the balance of each species?

Dougs are not especially well adapted for snowy climates. Their wide, round crowns do not shed snow as efficiently as the steeply sloped crowns of the firs, hemlocks, and spruces. Since the conical shape of evergreens is primarily adapted for snowy climates, mature Dougs tend to be rounder than other evergreens. When a space opens up on a slope facing south, the first new trees to move in are the Dougs. They are often the first colonizers in really brutal country, especially after a fire has swept over a slope facing south, but they also grow well with others. Dougs are always willing to leave wetter sites for the neighboring species that need more water.

PINE

Pines are distinguished from other evergreens by having needles attached in bundles and by utilizing animals for seed dispersal. Pine needle bundles, called **fascicles**, contain two, three, or five needles. Common two-needle pines are red, lodgepole, and jack pine. They are well adapted to grow on thin, sandy, or low-nutrient soils. Their trick is to spread their roots out horizontally along the surface of soil; even soil that is only 12" deep is infinitely wide. If you see a skinny evergreen growing out of a shear rock face, it's likely to be one of the two-needle pines. This group is fast growing, but short-lived. Rarely surpassing 300 years, the two-needle pines generally live 100 to 200 years.

Compared to other evergreens, the cones of pines are stiff, thick, and durable. Some cones, such as jack pine, are covered with a heavy resin that protects the seeds during fires. This type of cone, called **serotinous**, remains closed until the resin is melted by temperatures above about 120°F (35°C). In most but not all habitats, fire is the only way to achieve a temperature that high.

Pines are early invaders because they are sun-lovers, relatively intolerant of shade, and not very suitable to grow underneath other trees. Four other characteristics make them wonderful invaders, or pioneers: they are prolific, fast growing, tolerant of nutrient-poor sites, and self-pollinators. Self-pollination, the ability to fertilize their eggs with their own pollen, allows them to reproduce even when they are isolated on the edge of their habitat. Prolific means that they are sexually mature at a young age and produce many seeds.

The three common five-needled pines are white pine, white-bark pine, and limber pine. Whitebark grows at high altitudes, closer to the tree line than most other species. None of the five-needled pines are dominant in our forests today, mostly due to the blister rust epidemic that wiped them out in the 1950s. In the early 20th century, white pine, especially the eastern species, was the most important timber crop on the continent. The five-needled pine has relatively huge, and highly desirable, edible seeds, and thus are dispersed by animals.

HEMLOCK

Hemlock is recognized by its drooping terminal leader, a curled down top which makes the tree look like it's wearing a stocking cap. The tipped top sheds snow, much like the sloped roof of a house. It has long branches sweeping the ground. Ground-sweeping branches are hazardous in areas with frequent fires, so you shouldn't expect to find hemlocks in hot, dry places. In fact, hemlock is most at home in the wet, snowy, and moderate climates of the Pacific Northwest. Hemlock grows in forests along-side Douglas fir and redwoods, and also in the colder eastern forests. Hemlock needs less sunlight than its taller neighbors and fits in well just below the top canopy. Eastern hemlock (*Tsuga canadensis*) grows in the northern hardwoods forest with beech, birch, and maple.

LARCH

Larch, sometimes called tamarack, do not dominate any forest, but grow alongside the pines, fir, and spruce in the Rocky Mountains, the boreal forest, the Pacific Coast zone, and the eastern hardwoods. Larch needles are attached both singly and in bundles on spur shoots containing 12–20 needles. Larch is easily recognized in the fall and winter because it is deciduous. One species of larch is adapted to high altitude and grows right up to the tree line.

REDWOOD AND CEDAR

Redwoods, the tallest living things on Earth, can be 30 times as high as a single floor house (Figure 3.3). Shallow rooted and needing plenty of water, they grow only in the Pacific Coast forest zone. There they thrive in some of the mildest conditions

How Tall Can a Redwood Grow?

Gymnosperms, the giants of the plant kingdom, are undoubtedly the tallest living things on Earth. Why don't they just keep growing taller forever? Is there a limit to their height? Is it just a coincidence that they don't quite reach 400 feet (122 meters)?

While that might seem like a simple question for biologists to answer, it's only in the last couple of years that more light has been shed on the subject. George Koch of Northern Arizona University published his studies of Northern California redwoods in the journal *Nature*. His research, pinpointing four factors that limit the growth of redwoods and presumably all gymnosperms, estimates their maximum height to be about 420 feet (128 meters). The four factors are:

- Water flow
- Leaf density
- Photosynthesis
- Carbon dioxide concentration

Separately, each of these factors dwindles to its minimum level of efficiency when the tree reaches about 420 feet. Koch postulates that the combination of all factors reaching physiological limits may prevent trees from growing any taller. The only way that vital water can get to the top leaves on the tree is through capillary action from the roots. That's a long way, and the journey can take up to 24 days for the very tall trees.

For energy, trees need to get atmospheric carbon dioxide, which is absorbed through the leaves, and for photosynthesis, the trees also need sunlight. Clearly the need for sun stimulates the trees to continue their race to the sky, but as the tree gets taller, a proportionally higher number of leaves get left behind in the shade. Thus, height makes it less efficient to gather carbon dioxide and absorb sunlight.

Gymnosperms cannot grow taller indefinitely. What about the angiosperms? Think about the ancient live oaks. They grow wider but not taller as they age. In doing so, they have conceded the race to the sky to the gymnosperms. Perhaps cleverly, since ultimately it's a race that can't be won.

Figure 3.3 Someday you must find yourself looking up at a live redwood (*Sequoia sempervirens*), the tallest living thing that has ever inhabited our planet.

on the continent, the best place for trees to grow, and they are not likely to relinquish that location soon. Sensitive to salt spray, they can only grow inland. Individual trees cannot live forever, and a forest tree has to compete for sunlight by growing higher than its neighbors. Being tall comes with its difficulties. Soil is the only water source, and moving the water from the soil to the top of a 400-foot (122 meter) *Sequoia sempervirens* can take 24 days. That's about the limit for the species, so we won't be seeing redwoods much taller than that. Redwood heartwood produces chemicals that repel most insects, so that a felled redwood can remain on the forest floor for decades without significant decay.

Connections

Throughout the rest of the text we will refer to forest gymnosperms as evergreens, conifers, needle leafs, and the term newly introduced in this chapter, Coniferophyta. You should be familiar with all four of these terms, and the slight definitional differences. All conifers have cone-shaped crowns, but each genus has a distinct shape to its crown. The tip of the hemlock crown is soft and curls downward. The firs have narrow, needle-like crowns; scan the forest horizon for witches' hats and you'll find the firs. Spruce has elegant classic tops thick with (megasporangia) pinecones. The Douglas fir has a round crown that doesn't shed snow very well. Among conifers, the pines have the most widely spread and least conical tops.

The evergreens are generally the biggest and longest living forest trees. They were providing forest habitat on the planet for over 100 million years before the deciduous trees appeared. In our next chapter, we meet these deciduous newcomers, the angiosperms, and compare them to the evergreens.

I frequently tramped eight or ten miles through the deepest snow to keep an appointment with a beech-tree, or a yellow birch, or an old acquaintance among the pines.

— Henry David Thoreau

Trouble in the Forest:
Angiosperms

THE YOUNG FORESTS

In the last chapter, we met the elderly giants of the forest world—
gymnosperms—evergreens, kings of the plant world, the tallest
and oldest forest trees. Here, we meet the other class of trees, the
flowering plants—angiosperms—named *Magnoliophyta* after
the botanist P. Magnol. Magnoliophyta appeared on Earth only
120 million years ago. Many botanists consider their rapid expan-
sion to be one of the most significant events in **plant biogeography**,
the study of the distribution of plants across the globe. Considering the significant head start of the gymnosperms, you may
wonder how the angiosperms muscled into and established
themselves within the evergreen forests. There are two possible
explanations. Either magnoliophytes are able to colonize habitats
unavailable to gymnosperms, or they are able to displace the older
trees on their home turf.

First, let's ask whether it is possible that angiosperms can live
in habitat where evergreens cannot. Magnoliophyta are less
drought-tolerant than gymnosperms. Hence, the permafrost
tundra, with very little liquid surface water, although home to
evergreens, is inhospitable to flowering trees. Looking at forest
zones throughout the continent, we see that the flowering trees
have not colonized any habitat that was not already colonized
by the great evergreens. Therefore, dicot forest trees are thriving
because they can compete with and replace the evergreens on
their own turf. This happened almost everywhere except in the
coldest regions. What has given them the competitive advantage?

The basic innovation of the angiosperms is the angion, a
vessel that holds seeds and has helped propel the flowering trees
into plant world dominance. The seed vessel will eventually
develop into a fruit, a handy structure, as we'll see below, that
the gymnosperms lack. While gymnosperm seeds were all nearly
identical, the dicot trees exhibit a wide range of fascinating fruits
and pollination and dispersal strategies. Even though most dicot
tree seeds are wind dispersed like the evergreens, the former utilize

a more complex and varied wing mechanism to help the seed soar, fly, and whirl through the air.

The composition of angiosperm wood offers competitive advantage as well. Once thought to possess categorically harder wood than gymnosperms, we now know that this group includes some very soft-wooded species. Nevertheless, the hardest woods on the planet are angiosperms, and the softest are gymnosperms, so the nomenclature remains. Live oak produces the hardest wood in North America, followed by white oak, birch, beech, and sugar maple (Figure 4.1). All of the aforementioned are harder than longleaf pine, which is the hardest evergreen.

A categorical difference between the two classes of wood is that dicot wood has vessels in which to transport water, and gymnosperm wood does not. Gymnosperm trees transport water through tissue comprised of relatively long cells called tracheids. Tracheids are closed at both ends. The analogous cells in the angiosperm are open ended vessel members (sometimes called vessel elements) that when stacked end to end form vessels. Vessels are to tracheids as a straw is to a sponge. Using vessels, the dicots can transport water many times faster than the soft-wood gymnosperms. The younger and most efficient trees can move water 100 times faster than softwood—the average is 10 times faster. Still, there is a seasonal water shortage, mostly due to the frozen winter ground, that evergreens combat by utilizing needle-like leaves that do not lose water to transpiration very rapidly. Angiosperms adapt to the seasonal water shortage by shedding their leaves and entering dormancy.

WHERE ARE THE HARDWOOD DOMINATED FORESTS?

The hardwoods probably evolved in subtropical and dry climates, and gradually spread north. Hence, they are not prolific in Canada. Hardwoods dominate the eastern U.S., blending into the oak-pine mixed forest along the Atlantic and Gulf Coasts. A relatively narrow belt of hardwood forest follows the bottomlands

Figure 4.1 Live oak exhibits some classic angiosperm features. Note the broadleaves and the decurrent growth pattern of relatively thick horizontal branches.

of the Mississippi River. Although younger than evergreens, they cannot compete well in very cold regions, where evergreens still hold the physiological advantage. While the evergreens are capable of photosynthesis in the winter, the broadleaf forests are dormant.

Angiosperm trees are not without weaknesses, so in order to thrive they have had to choose their battles carefully. You can see that North America's broadleaf forests all inhabit mid-latitudes of the **temperate zone**. Hot summers, cold winters, and moderate shoulder seasons characterize the temperate zone, the area between the Tropic of Capricorn (23°30' south of the equator) and the Tropic of Cancer (23°30' north of the equator). All the North American dicot dominated forests are east of the Great Plains and south of the taiga. These areas are not too cold and not too dry.

Living is easy in the temperate zone, not just for trees, but also for fungi, a severe pathogen on the hardwoods. The Rocky Mountain and the boreal forests are relatively immune to fungal infections that often spread like wildfire through the southern hardwood forests. The most heavily affected zones are the warmest: the southern oak-pine forest and the southern Florida rainforest.

WHAT ARE THE MAIN CHARACTERISTICS OF FORESTS?

Again, we'll consider common groups of trees, since forests don't work well when consisting of single species. The northern hardwoods forest is sometimes called the beech-birch-maple-hemlock forest, since these four species dominate (Figure 4.2). Common associations are beech, birch, and maple; oak and hickory in the drier areas; beech and maple; maple and basswood; and oak and chestnut.

Recall that angiosperm trees are dicots, as opposed to gymnosperm seeds, which contain many cotyledons. Again as opposed to gymnosperms, dicot species may be dioecious, carrying pollen and eggs on separate trees. Dicot trees are generally smaller, shorter, and shorter-lived than gymnosperms. They shed their leaves in the fall, and tend toward a decurrent shape. The dicot flower consists of **stamens**, which produce and carry pollen and an ovary (carpel) within the **pistil**, which contains the ovules or eggs. If a single flower includes both pistil and stamen, it is a **perfect flower** (Figure 4.3). A flower that contains only pistils is a pistillate flower, and one with only stamen is a staminate flower—both types are considered imperfect. **Imperfect flowers** are a common characteristic among eastern dicot trees.

Figure 4.2 Birch (A) is recognized by its white bark. Maple (B) is a slender tree often inhabiting the subcanopy. Beech (C) a large tree enjoying full sun, its easy to see how it can dominate a canopy.

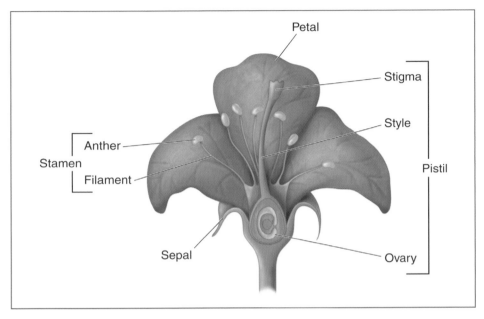

Figure 4.3 Flowers use color, scent, and shape to attract pollinators to the stamen, where pollen is produced, and the stigma, the receptive area where pollen grains germinate.

We will discuss the special features and adaptations of the following six genera of forest hardwoods:

1. poplar (*Populus*)

2. maple (*Acer*)

3. beech (*Fagus*)

4. oak (*Quercus*)

5. hickory (*Carya*)

6. birch (*Betula*)

There are only two common forest species of birch in North America. Yellow birch *(Betula alleghaniensis)* is an important component of both the beech-birch-maple-hemlock and the central hardwood zones. River birch (*Betula nigra*) grows in the bottomlands of the Mississippi Delta. Birch boasts a thin, shiny bark that easily peels off in horizontal strips. Its fruit consists of tiny cones less than one inch (2.54 cm) long. Birch tolerates shade and likes moist ground, has imperfect flowers, and grows to 100 feet (30 meters), with a two-foot (60 cm) diameter.

MAPLE

Maples prefer wet sites and tolerate shade a bit better than sun-loving oaks. A large genus, there are nearly 200 species worldwide and over a dozen common in North America's forests. Maples have a wide variety of leaf shapes, but all species share a common fruit type, the **samara**, consisting of an attached pair of nuts each with its own long wing. Maple trees are essentially absent from Rocky Mountain and boreal forests. Most western maples are really shrubs. The only maple species west of the Great Plains, big leaf maple (*Acer macrophylium*), thrives in the Pacific Coast forest. As we said earlier about the Pacific Coast forest zone, most trees are bigger there than anywhere else in their range and this is likely to be true of the maple as well. The largest maples in North America live in the evergreen forests of the Pacific Coast. Still, even at a maximum height of 100 feet (30 meters) tall, they must live in the conifers' shadows.

The tallest maple species, reaching about 120 feet (37 meters), is the sugar maple (*Acer saccharum*), which is the foundation of the maple syrup industry and the single most economically important maple in the northern hardwoods zone. In the central hardwoods, sugar and red maple (*Acer rubra*) are found together, and in the bottomland hardwood forests of the Mississippi delta, box elder (*Acer negundo*) is the prominent maple.

BEECH AND OAK

Chestnuts, beech, and oak are members of the Fagaceae family. Fagaceae, meaning "good to eat," is an appropriate name since

Ginseng

Hardwood forests provide an important crop, ginseng. Ginseng (*Panax quinquefolium*) grows only along undisturbed forest floors beneath a canopy of hardwoods. Like wild ginger, ginseng also has a 4,000-year-old Chinese tradition heralding its value as a medicine.

The wild harvested plant has been a significant part of the economy of North America's eastern hardwoods ever since the arrival of the Europeans. Ginseng was one of New York's most important forest crops in the early 1900s. Eventually, a fungal pathogen destroyed nearly the entire population.

Although it may grow on tree farms, wild ginseng currently brings in about 1–2 orders of magnitude more gross profit than the cultivated plant. Basic economics would imply that the cost difference is due to the larger over-head on the wild plant; the net profits should be comparable. But for plant poachers who steal ginseng, there is no overhead.

Poaching is a main part of the ginseng controversy. While the government may consider ginseng harvesters to be poachers, Americans have been har-vesting the crop from forest lands for 300 years and do not consider themselves poachers. Are they? To what extent should people be allowed to glean material from national forests? After all, trees are commonly logged on public forest land.

Further complicating the picture, researchers published in *Science* (2004) evidence that wild deer threaten the ginseng crop. They appear to be devouring it. The researchers suggested bringing back the natural predators of the deer: mountain lion, coyote, wolf, and bear. But there are at least two sides to the deer issue. Some citizens, mostly those that sell ginseng, are interpreting the data as a call to increase human hunting in order to eliminate deer from the hardwoods.

Isn't one of the roles of a forest to support wildlife? What kinds of wildlife should be supported? Deer are part of the forest, and bear and other carnivores used to be a part of the forest. What would your position be as a forester?

the edible fruits of the family are an important food source. When Europeans settled North America, the chestnut tree, reaching 100 feet (30 meters), was the tallest in the eastern hardwoods forest zone. Around 1900, citizens of the U.S., probably in New York, imported ornamental chestnut trees from Asia. A lethal fungus on the imported trees spread rapidly. Commonly called chestnut blight, this fungus killed three and a half billion American chestnut trees in 40 years. Although chestnuts are nearly extinct in the eastern forests, beech nuts and oak acorns remain an important food source for wildlife.

Only one species of beech, American beech (*Fagus grandifolia*), grows in North America's forests where it can be found in both the beech-birch-maple mixed group and in the central hardwoods. We recognize beech by its smooth, thin bark and fruit consisting of nuts enclosed in a bur. Growing up to 150 feet (46 meters), beech prefers moist, rich soil and tolerates shade.

There are over 500 species of oak (*Quercus*; hereafter abbreviated *Q.*) worldwide of which 15 are common in North American forests. Oak is so prevalent in the central broadleaf zone that we sometimes think of that as an oak forest. The oaks exhibit a wide diversity of leaf shapes and habitat preferences, but all shed their seed in the distinct acorn fruit, and are strongly decurrent with very broad crowns. All oaks have grey furrowed bark, prefer dry or well-drained sites, and like plenty of sun. The tallest trees rarely get above 100 feet (30 meters). Among dicots, oaks are famous for being long-lived, possessing a very long, deep taproot, and having a very hard (dense) wood. Oaks bear the male and female reproductive parts on two separate flowers, both growing on a single tree, thus they are monoecious. The pollen-producing flowers are all catkins.

The only significant oak tree west of the plains is Kelloggs (*Q. kelloggii*), which grows in the hot southern California climate. Red oak (*Q. rubra*) is the only species common to the northern hardwoods. The other 13 tree species are southeastern. Live oaks (*Q. virginiana*), short trees that seem to have a limitless horizontal spread, are adapted to salt spray and live along the Atlantic Coast. Live oaks retain their leaves throughout much of the winter, shedding their old leaves as the new annual leaves appear, and are an example of an evergreen angiosperm.

HICKORY

Some species of hickory grow on dry, sunny sites throughout the oak-pine community, while other species inhabit moist and somewhat shady sites along river bottoms, within the central hardwood forest. Walnut-sized fruit in a hard, smooth shell identifies the hickory. All species have edible nuts, but some are very bitter. Those that are sweet provide, along with oak, a critical food source in the eastern forests.

POPLAR

Cottonwood and aspen are both poplars that produce soft wood, softer than many evergreens, and inhabit sunny, sometimes disturbed sites. Quaking aspen (*Populus tremuloides*) has the widest range of any forest tree in North America, occurring coast to coast and from northern Canada to the coastline of the Gulf of Mexico. Producing small seeds, aspen often reproduces vegetatively, forming large clone groups that may survive for over a thousand years (Figure 4.4).

BROADLEAF AND NEEDLELEAF

In the forest zones dominated by Coniferophyta—boreal, Pacific Coast, and the Rocky Mountain—deciduous trees are truly uncommon, however, they do exist. The taiga is interspersed with aspen and birch, although many only grow to shrub height. Bigleaf maples grow throughout the Pacific zone. Oaks thrive along the coast and in the drier forests of California. At high elevations, and in the northern part of the Rocky Mountains, quaking aspens are not unusual.

Figure 4.4 Fall is one of the easiest times to identify aspen clones. Their inherited color patterns belie the suspicious nature of their roots. Based on color and size, there appear to be sets of trees that are twins. These pairs and triplets are probably not siblings or separate trees, but are members of a clonal group. These clones are genetically identical organisms produced from shoot growth off the parent and not from the seed.

Connections

Angiosperms are young, restless, wild, and flamboyant. Angiosperms first appear in the fossil record over 100 million years *after* the gymnosperm giants had spread throughout the habitable world. In that relatively short time, these flowering trees have blossomed into over 300,000 species of amazing variation. The large, old, and unwavering gymnosperms have never produced more than 1,000 different species. The angiosperms, latecomers, came to dominate most of the plant world within 30 million years. This takeover of the plant world by angiosperms is thought by many plant biologists to be the single most important botanical event in the history of our planet.

Angiosperms have many more tricks for adapting to a changing world than the gymnosperms. Most importantly, they have flowers to lure a variety of pollinators to their bidding, and they cradle their seeds in a carpel, which becomes another bait mechanism for seed dispersers—a fruit. Some dicots even have specialized male and female trees. Angiosperms have a dense wood with vessels to suck water at very fast rates, but when water freezes in the winter, they drop their leaves and rest until spring.

The angiosperms are a family of aliases. Throughout the text we will refer to a forest angiosperm as a hardwood, dicot, broadleaf, and Magnoliophyta, the term introduced in this chapter. You should be comfortable with all four of these nearly interchangeable terms and be aware of the slight differences in meaning.

With all the advantages and complexities, the North American dicots still yield all but the temperate forests to the gymnosperms. The giant, long-lived evergreens had a head start during the Ice Age since they were better able to colonize the land in the wake of the retreating ice. The Ice Age spruce genus still rules the boreal forest, and the evergreen rules over the Pacific Northwest. The dicots are common forest shrub species, as we shall see in the next chapter.

We have now considered the trees separately and need to put them together into the forest and examine the dynamics that occur when groups of trees of different ages, sizes, talents, and complaints all come together under one roof—the forest canopy.

5 The Forest Family Tree:
Intra-forest Dynamics

An elaborate mythology of trees exists
across a broad range of ancient cultures.
— Sacred Places: Trees and the Sacred

The Forest Family Tree:
Intra-forest Dynamics

Forests are seldom static but evolve with time. In the southeastern U.S., the oak-pine forests are *supposed* to be hardwood forests. That is, the habitat and zone type is considered by ecologists to be hardwood, not oak-pine. In Minnesota, red and white pine forests of the last century are today balsam fir, spruce, and hardwood. In northwest Wyoming, the stands of spruce and fir from 15 years ago are now mostly Douglas fir. The true firs failed to recover from fire.

In northern Montana, red cedar backbones are hidden under the eaves of the Douglas fir, and provide vast nursery beds for the seeds of the prolific and skinny lodgepole. Yet there hasn't been any young red cedar in at least 50 years. An 80-year-old neighbor recalls the cedar forest at the turn of the 20th century. Does your family tree record the history of trees in your forest?

We know that a forest is a biological community dominated by trees. We also know that these are not always the same species of trees; we have looked at several different forest zones in North America, each with a different composition of tree species in a different pattern of dominance. But even *within* each forest, the relative dominance of tree species is not constant. Forests change in two dimensions: time and space. Over time, one group of species thins out, possibly even becoming rare, while another group increases to take its place. The community losing dominance may become so scarce that its only representation in the forest is within the seed bank. How long does this take? You can probably guess that the period is related to the life span of the trees in the community. Eastern hardwoods don't live as long as western conifers so we'd expect turnover to be faster in the east. A quick turnover would be hundreds of years. Some western species, redwoods, for example, can dominate a forest for a thousand years or more.

The pattern that forms as one community succeeds or replaces another is called **succession** and is sometimes preceded by **disturbance**. A disturbance in the ecological sense is an event that clears away one community to make space for another. Both succession and disturbance are important factors in temporal forest community changes that we will consider in this chapter.

In addition to temporal dynamics, forests vary in vertical space, from the roots at the bottom to the canopy. We will examine three different vertical zones: the forest floor, the subcanopy, and the canopy. According to the Smithsonian Tropical Research Institute, a major sponsor of canopy studies, the term *canopy* is used by different researchers to mean different things. While it is clear that the forest has a vertical dimension, individual researchers divide the canopy into few or many compartments. An all-inclusive definition is that the canopy is all foliage, twigs, and branches above the ground. Other researchers find it useful to subdivide the canopy into vertical sections. Here we define the canopy as the *topmost* contiguous layer. We will consider trees and shrubs whose crowns do not reach the topmost layer of the forest to be part of the subcanopy. The crowns of the trees and shrubs in the subcanopy do not receive any direct sunlight.

SUCCESSION

The temporal dimension of the forest is as varied as the spacial. Don't look for a concise definition of succession in the glossary, because you won't find one. Scientists are unclear how to define succession, beyond the general understanding that it is a change of species composition over time. Certainly the species dominating a forest community will change over time; evidence is prolific. But what is the nature and cause of the change? Succession is a complex issue, clouded by our inability to discover whether it has an endpoint community, known as a **climax community**, or whether succession itself continues indefinitely. Ecologists are still conducting experiments and looking for evidence as to whether climax communities exist.

Succession is an ordered change that is inherent in any forest. Whether or not it ends, it follows a pattern and is to some extent predictable. Pattern and predictability separate succession from disturbance. Predictions are made based on the adaptations of the current composition of trees. For example, a forest in the northern Rockies at elevations between 7,000 and 7,500 feet (2,134 and 2,286 meters) will consist of white-bark pine, fir, spruce, and lodgepole pine, with varying densities and various numbers of individuals of each species. One event that will alter the relative densities of each species is fire. Following a fire, lodgepole pine tends to increase relative to other species. Conversely, excessive rainfall over a long period will favor the spruce. Long-term drought will encourage the spruce to die back and the pines will again increase relative to

Forest Canopy

Many ecologists study just the canopy layer of the forest which is a new development. It is only since the 1990s that canopy science has emerged as a focus within forest science. One reason this science has been slow to develop is the problematic logistics of working in the canopy. How do you get there? Nowadays, ecologists use permanently installed towers and cranes that reach between 140 and 185 feet (42 and 56 meters). Due to the complexity of studying the canopy, research would be prohibitively expensive except for the establishment of permanent field stations complete with miles of ropes and pulleys, canopy platforms, and towers. The Smithsonian Institution built the world's first canopy crane in Panama in 1990. Several years later, a canopy research crane was built in the Wind Rivers Experimental Forest near Washington's Columbia River. Today, there are 11 cranes scattered all over the world in both temperate and tropical forest canopies.

If the physical adventure alone isn't enough to entice you into this new field, consider the importance of the forest roof. The roof is the layer with the most exposure to sunlight, so most of the ecosystem's the other species. Heavy snows and cold weather favor fir, spruce, and whitebark pine.

Which of those combinations of species is a stage in the series of changes, called a **seral stage**, and which is the climax community? To find the climax community, ask yourself, *"Can these trees reproduce themselves, perpetuating this forest indefinitely, in the absence of disturbance?"* Many times you will answer *"No. The dominant trees cannot reproduce under their own canopy."* The main reason for this is that the canopy provides shade and if parent trees are shade intolerant, then their young cannot survive beneath them. The sun-loving, two-needled pines, such as lodgepole and jack pine, are therefore

photosynthesis, hence energy production, happens within the canopy. Following the energy flow, most of the species in a forest, including plants, animals, fungi, and bacteria, sequester themselves in the canopy. Finally, epiphytes, a class of plants sometimes called air plants, live on top of other plants in the canopy. Without rooting in the soil, they must receive their nutrients from the air. Epiphytes, common in tropical and subtropical canopies, include orchids and ferns. When we consider the interface between living things and our atmosphere, we find that up to 90% occurs in the canopy, which is justifiably assumed to influence the world's climate.

Before you decide to join up, you may ask yourself, *"What kind of information have these treetop-dwelling ecologists brought us?"* A recent study has demonstrated some species of hardwoods grow root systems into the canopy layer to absorb the nutrients afforded by dead and decaying epiphytes. Current research focuses on climate effects, carbon cycling, and the complex net of interactions among canopy plants, insects, and spiders.

not able to perpetuate themselves once they take over the canopy. Instead, they are dependent on disturbance, and therefore they are not part of a climax community.

DISTURBANCE

Climax communities are stable in the *absence* of disturbance. They withstand small perturbations some of the time, and other times disturbance causes them to cede the forest to a serial stage. Disturbance differs from succession primarily by being unpredictable, and neither cyclic nor inherent in the forest. Although not predictable, disturbance events are common, and often become necessary for new communities to overthrow the climax community. Wind, disease, fire, pollution, and insect predation are the most common forest disturbances. Perhaps these events sound dreadful and many are, in fact, cataclysmic. However, *disturbance* is a scientific term without associated moral judgment. It is neither a good nor a bad event. We will discuss fire, the most critical event in turning around serial stages in many of North America's forest, in Chapter 8. Insect predation is discussed in Chapter 7.

Unlike fires and plant-ravaging animals, wind events (sustained speeds of 100 miles per hour, or 161 kilometers per hour) are generally small and avoid attention, though as a forest disturbance, they are omnipresent. One interesting wind event of the previous decade occurred in the Boundary Waters Canoe Are Wilderness (BWCAW) near the border of Canada and Minnesota. In July 1999, a three-mile-wide stretch of this boreal forest was flattened in one of the largest blowdowns in the recorded history of North America. Analyzing the aftermath of this blowdown, which occurred in a popular recreation area, will involve teams of scientists for decades to come. Initial concern was that within 8 to 12 years post-blowdown, the millions of dead and dying trees would invite cataclysmic wild fire. However, only five years after the event, feasting fungi

Figure 5.1 The blowdown in Minnesota's Boundary Water Canoe Area Wilderness (BWCAW) happened in 1999 and may be the largest windthrow event in the history of North America's forests.

have consumed a significant amount of the potential fuel, and the anticipated fires have remained at bay. Most of the windthrown trees are Pinaceae, specifically pine, spruce, and fir, all of which are slower to recover from windthrow than hardwoods. A possible reason is that Pinaceae reproduction, unlike some oaks and poplars for example, is seed dependent. Seeds, and the birds required to disperse them, become scarce following wind events.

Even in the absence of the anticipated fire, we have witnessed succession in the BWCAW blowdown (Figure 5.1). Perhaps because of their relatively small diameter, fir trees were killed in greater proportion than their neighboring red and white pines, which are now enjoying increased space in the forest. In other words, the disturbance allowed pine to succeed fir.

Plant diseases, both imported and indigenous, disturb vast areas in our forests. Blister rust and chestnut blight are two of the most important and incurable epidemics in recorded history (Figure 5.2). Both are caused by nonnative fungal pathogens brought to North America in the 1900s. Blister rust began its rapid spread in the 1950s by attacking five-needled pines, which happen to produce some of the continent's most economically valuable wood. Several of these species, for example, white and whitebark pine, are key elements of the forests where they occur, effecting virtually every living thing in their community. Since the rust is a parasite, it is not self-sufficient and cannot survive on its own. The organisms upon which it is dependent are called hosts. Blister rust has two types of hosts: pine trees, which it kills, and *Ribes*, which it doesn't. *Ribes* is a genus of berry-producing plants including red and black currents and gooseberries.

The American government tried to fight the disease with "rust-busters," squads of men who would attack and kill any *Ribes* plant within sight of a five-needled pine. The plan effectively wiped out the berries but the pines continued to die until, nearly extinct, the government's rust-busting army surrendered to the Asian fungus. A decade too late, it was discovered that the

Figure 5.2 Bright orange blister rust fungus, an exotic invader, is still visible in natural forests wherever you find five-needle pines.

lethal fungal **spores**, reproductive cells that do not need to be fertilized in order to produce a new being (fungus reproduce with spore instead of seed), spread hundreds of miles from the *Ribes* plant, so killing berries adjacent to pines could not save them; they were being killed by infested *Ribes* many miles away. Today, our forests remain wanting for the missing white, white-bark, and limber pines. Although not extinct, they are making only a slow comeback, while the blister rust spores still blow through the western winds.

Chestnut blight forever changed the composition of the eastern hardwood forests, killing over a billion chestnut trees by 1940. Chestnut, once the tallest tree in its forest zone, now survives only as a stunted shrub. Like the blister rust, chestnut blight persists unabated.

Disturbances come in many degrees of severity; we even use the term to refer to the fall of a single tree in a forest. Though you might not hear it fall, that single tree is in fact creating a disturbance. When a disturbance completely wipes out a forest ecosystem—not merely one community, but the entire forest— life must begin anew with **primary succession**, the rebuilding of a system from scratch. Primary succession often rebuilds with buried seeds and soil organisms. An example is the Ice Age glaciers erasing the forests of the Pacific Northwest. Unlike glaciers, forest fires and disease outbreaks alter the relative species composition but do not obliterate the entire ecosystem. The community changes that follow this lesser disturbance are called **secondary succession**.

CHANGES THROUGH SPACE

We categorize forests according to the tallest and most obtrusive trees in the canopy, but these trees may not be the most common in terms of either number of individuals or **biomass** (the total weight of all the representatives of a given species in a given area). For example, in an oak-pine forest, it's quite likely that if you calculated the total number of plants for each represented species, oaks and pines together would not comprise the majority. There are many plant species that are neither in the canopy nor on their way to becoming so, but instead belong to one of the other vertical components of the forest. The standard vertical compartments of a forest are canopy, midcanopy, and floor.

When a giant redwood falls, the composition of the canopy, midcanopy, and forest floor are all affected. The hole in the canopy allows light and water to reach a new group of trees. These shorter trees making use of that light aspire to grow into the canopy and begin the process of competition and only one will be successful. Crashing to the forest floor, the redwood has torn and crushed the shrubs below. Shade-tolerant species, they will be replaced with sun lovers. Finally, the redwood comes to rest upon the forest floor, providing nutrients and a large source of carbon for the benefit of the bottom-dwelling organisms and plants.

Subcanopy trees receive less light, water, and pollinator attention than their taller neighbors. Survival in the subcanopy is not easy; the successful shrubs are shade tolerant and often rely on crawling rather than flying animals for pollination. Some important members of the subcanopy in western forests are yew (*Taxus*) and juniper (*Juniperus*). Yews are happy growing in the shade, but the sun-seeking junipers are frustrated. Juniper uses a few tricks for getting rid of some annoying shade; they nuzzle up against the lodgepole. The lodgepole, of course, has cleverly shed its lower branches to increase its fire resistance. So the juniper foils the lodgepole's attempt at fire resistance by filling the space where the lower branches would be. When fires come through, the highly flammable juniper acts as kindling and the pine torches make room for the offspring of the juniper. Many times the subcanopy juniper will survive the fire; it is generally resistant unless the fire completely burns over its top.

One of the commonly misunderstood forest shrubs is the mistletoe. True mistletoe (*Phorodendron*), the wood from which Cupid's arrows are crafted, is a common component of the hardwood forests and, unlike the dwarf mistletoes (*Arceuthobium*) of the evergreen forests, is not pathogenic. When it is young, dwarf mistletoe looks like a fungus, but it's merely a native shrub in disguise.

Important components of the forest floor are **litter**, **duff**, ground cover, and nurse logs. Litter is the organic material in the carpet; for example, needles, dead grasses, and pinecones. Once the litter begins to decompose, it consolidates into a layer known as duff. Due to the decaying leaf litter, duff is a thick layer in the hardwood forests; you can even roll it up. In some evergreen forests, the duff is only one-third inch (0.85 centimeters) thick or less. There are two main reasons for this difference. Evergreens shed their needle leaves only once every 3 to 19 years, depending on the species. Secondly, the evergreen forests tend to be colder and drier and thus less hospitable to decomposing organisms.

There is another significant difference between the deciduous and the evergreen forest floor. Deciduous forests experience drastic seasonal light changes. In the fall, after the leaves drop, plenty of light reaches the floor of the deciduous forest. In the spring, when the leaves begin to grow, that light begins to dwindle. Perennial shrubs, which have most of their photosynthetic and water transport machinery in place, can flower while there is still sun, but this is too great a task for an annual plant that must build up its resources from scratch every year. This is why perennials dominate the floor of the deciduous forest, while evergreen forests are more inviting to annuals.

Nurse logs, present on the floor of natural forests, illustrate another difference between tree farms and forests. When a tree dies, it becomes a bedding site where seeds of other plants or even its own offspring can sprout. The older a forest is, the more likely that it will have nurse logs along the forest floor. The number of nurse logs per unit area is sometimes used to help define an old growth forest.

Connections

A forest is an ecosystem that changes through time and space. Succession occurs primarily because mature forest trees create an ecosystem into which their own offspring cannot succeed. Therefore, the offspring of another tree species will succeed. The declining species may cycle back to a position of dominance in the future. If the cycle stops and stabilizes, it is said that a climax community exists.

By definition, no forest community is stable in the face of disturbance. Regular disturbances that interrupt the natural series of community stages and prevent climax communities from forming include avalanches, fire, and disease.

In addition to temporal variability, forests have an internal vertical structure. When visiting forests, there are three zones you should observe. From a distance, the most obvious layer is the canopy. Once you enter the forest, two new worlds await you: the subcanopy and the floor. The drier, colder forests will be sparser in these areas, and some will have floor so bare that they look like they've been mowed into parkland. Others will house a hundred different species in a square meter.

This chapter should confirm your understanding of the vast differences between a tree farm/plantation and a forest. Can you see that neither succession nor vertical variation occurs on a tree farm? Can you understand that "disturbance" would not be a neutral, but rather a pejorative expression on a tree farm?

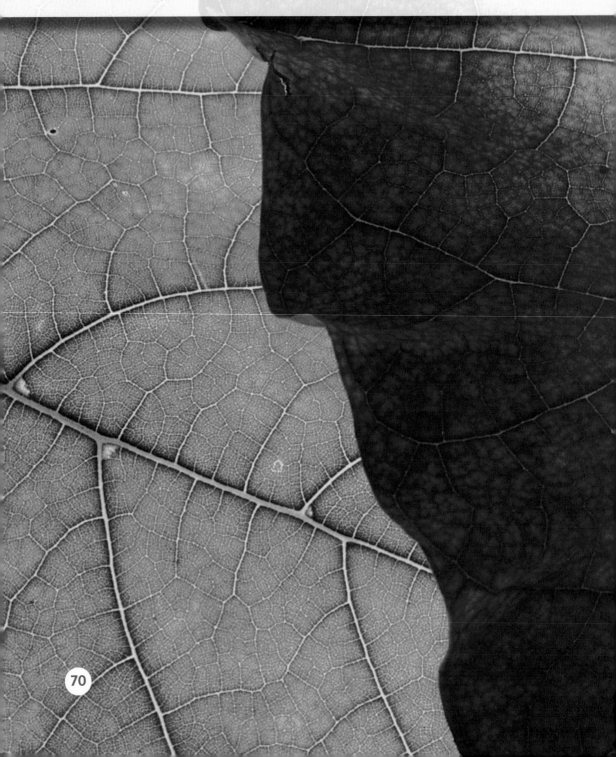

6 Thinking Like a Forest:
Ecology

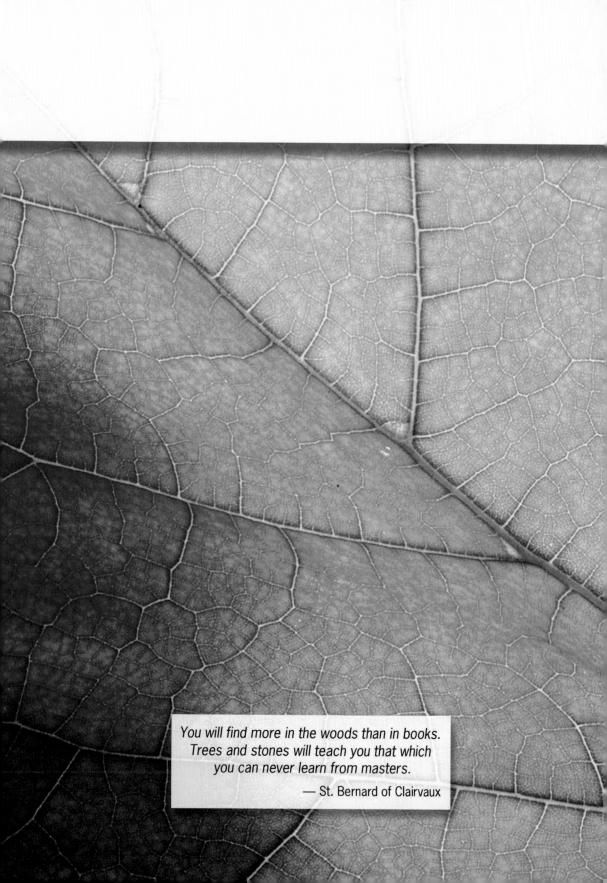

*You will find more in the woods than in books.
Trees and stones will teach you that which
you can never learn from masters.*

— St. Bernard of Clairvaux

Thinking Like a Forest:
Ecology

Scientists today readily accept the idea that forests are ecosystems and that studying forests is tantamount to studying ecology. Those statements seem obvious to us now, but in industrial America prior to the 1950s studying forestry meant learning how to cut down trees. Foresters learned how to plant, grow, and shield trees from fires and insects. They learned about maximizing profit when harvesting trees. Today, we might find that studying forestry simply to become a tree farmer is as odd as studying zoology simply to become a chef. The industrial world has expanded its view of natural resources beyond mere utilization. We have taken the separate compartments of nature and humans and collapsed them into a whole functioning system. If you had to choose one word to explain how and why the change occurred, it would be: *Odum.*

In 1953, Dr. Eugene Odum published *Fundamentals of Ecology,* the book credited with changing our assumptions about the natural world. Dr. Odum's term *ecosystem* has changed our perception of nature, and changed the way we study the biological world (Figure 6.1). In Chapter 1, we learned that a forest is magic because it is greater than the sum of its parts. There are many ways to convey this concept. The words *gestalt* and *synergy* both describe the quality of being more than the sum of one's parts. Regardless of how you choose to say it, there is but one implication: the forest is a house. Dr. Odum told us that the flow of necessary commodities keeps the various members of the house dependant upon each other. Commodities passing within the house and between the house and the outside world include water, nutrients, and energy. Notice that these essentials are not living things, but are instead part of the physical world. Odum was able to visualize the connection between the living (biotic) and the nonliving (abiotic) world because his close collaborator, his brother, was a physical scientist. The Odum brothers, biologist and physicist, tied the abiotic and biotic worlds together in an intricate web. Forest ecology is the study

Figure 6.1 Dr. Eugene Odum (1913–2002) the father of modern ecology is seen here. Through his eyes the world saw a new pattern in the relationship between the abiotic and biotic communities.

of the forest ecosystem, the interrelationships between biotic and abiotic.

WHAT ARE THE CHARACTERISTICS OF AN ECOSYSTEM?

Ecosystem is a concept, not an object. A concept has characteristics but not a precise definition. For example, "love" and "justice" are concepts not objects, and, like ecosystem, we cannot precisely define them, so instead we describe them. Like love and justice, the description of ecosystem has inspired many volumes of text and will no doubt inspire many more.

In a nutshell, Dr. Odum tells us that ecosystems are areas of unspecified boundaries that share a flow of energy, water, and nutrients. Water is critical because life is not possible in its absence. Forests need water and nutrients, especially carbon and nitrogen, in order to grow. Since trees are continually dying, they must be replaced, so a forest that is not growing by replacing trees is essentially a forest that is dying.

What about energy? For most of the living world, the main source of energy is the sun. Only organisms capable of photosynthesis can use the power of the sun directly. The rest of us use the sun indirectly. We are dependent upon other living things to supply us with food and oxygen.

THE WATER CYCLE

Water is a limiting factor in the presence of forests. This means that the availability of water, its quality and quantity, is enough to determine whether or not a forest can exist in any given location. Like all plants, forests need water to grow because it is a vital ingredient in the process of photosynthesis, and because individual plant cells are composed largely of water.

You are certainly familiar with the term "the water cycle." This refers to the fact that all the water in the universe is by necessity used and reused. This is because all of the water that will ever exist is here already. Our planet cannot produce any more water than what we have right now. The water on the planet is therefore a closed system. Think about filling a jar with water and screwing on the lid. You can put the jar in the freezer, you can heat it on a stove, and you can turn it sideways and shake it around, but the quantity of water inside that jar won't increase or decrease.

It is not just the presence of water, but also its quality that affects forests. Trees are very particular when it comes to their water. The water must be in liquid form and it must not be too acidic or alkaline. Trees cannot survive on either ice or steam which is why trees do not grow on permafrost or inside hot springs basins that consist only of steam vents. Acidity results from a high concentration of hydrogen atoms; alkalinity from a low concentration. Acidity and alkalinity are measured on the pH scale, with 1 representing the highest level of acidity (highest hydrogen concentration), and 14 representing the lowest levels or *alkaline* concentrations (lowest hydrogen concentration). One of the most important discoveries of the last century was that forests die in the presence of highly acidic water. Acidic water in the soil causes harm in two ways. First, the acidity robs the forest soil of nutrients by dissolving and then washing away calcium, potassium, and magnesium. Second, acidity poisons the soil by releasing harmful metals such as aluminum into a form in which they are readily taken up by trees. Free aluminum, when absorbed by trees, may stunt root growth. Other metals released by acid include lead, mercury, zinc, copper, cadmium, and chromium, all of which may slow tree growth or kill associated bacteria necessary for nitrogen uptake. Acid rain causes damage even if it never reaches the soil. Leaves exposed to an acidic fog lose nutrients, then weaken and succumb to drought or frost.

The basic circular route of water on Earth is from the atmosphere, where it condenses and falls as rain, to the ground, where it is consumed by plants, animals, and other living things. Animals and people return water to the atmosphere with every exhalation. But exhalation is an insignificant amount compared to the vast quantities of water cycled by trees in the process of transpiration.

THE NITROGEN CYCLE

Nitrogen, a nonmetallic chemical element, is essential for the growth and survival of the forest. An element is the basic unit of matter. Any substance that cannot be broken down into a simpler one by a chemical reaction is an element. You will find the chart of all 92 naturally occurring elements in any chemistry textbook. Nitrogen is one of 17 elements that serve as plant nutrients. In fact, along with sulfur, potassium, calcium, phosphorus, and magnesium, nitrogen is a macronutrient because it is essential for living things. Like water, the presence of nitrogen is a limiting factor in plant growth and exists in the universe in only finite amounts. We all take, use, and return nitrogen to the common pool. Forest trees need nitrogen in order to produce proteins. Trees have many uses for proteins, for example, to transport water and minerals in their cells, and to store and produce growth hormones. Nitrogen is also an essential part of DNA, the hereditary material contained within each cell. Every new plant cell produced must include a packet of DNA. If you recall that pines are adapted to poor quality soils, meaning soil low in nitrogen and other nutrients, it should not surprise you that hardwood forests are more dependent upon nitrogen than evergreen forests.

Nitrogen cycles through the ecosystem in two forms: gas and solid. The gaseous form, along with oxygen and carbon dioxide, is common in the atmosphere, but cannot be directly absorbed by trees. Trees require nitrogen that is both solid and chemically bound to either oxygen or hydrogen, for example, as nitrate or ammonia.

Only a few species of bacteria and fungi can bind or "fix" atmospheric nitrogen and convert it to a form that can be taken up by plants. Too small to be seen with the naked eye, these bacteria and fungi are collectively called nitrogen-fixing microorganisms. Some bacteria live independently in the soil but may, upon receiving chemical signals from plants, attach themselves to tree roots and form nodules.

These microorganisms provide most of the nitrogen needs of the forest trees. However, there are two other sources of nitrogen: rainfall and litter (Figure 6.2). Atmospheric nitrogen travels through rainfall to the forest floor. Parts of the plant bodies that

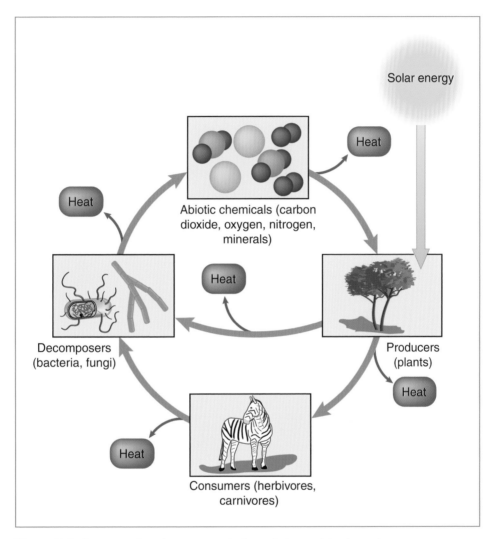

Figure 6.2 An ecosystem is composed of nonliving nutrients and energy resources, producers that draw from these resources, and consumers that get their energy from the producers. Decomposers then break down leaf litter and wastes into nutrients that can be cycled through the ecosystem again.

die and slough off also accumulate on the forest floor, collectively referred to as litter. Proteins and other molecules in the plant litter contain nitrogen. The nitrogen in these proteins is usually bound to carbon molecules, making it impossible for the roots to absorb. Living in the soil, litter decomposers such as fungi free the nitrogen from the carbon so that it can reenter the cycle.

THE CARBON CIRCLE

Like nitrogen, most of the carbon necessary for life comes from the atmosphere. However, trees don't depend on microorganisms to fix carbon, they do it themselves. Green plants absorb atmospheric carbon dioxide and create a form of carbon that other organisms can use. In other words, plants *fix* carbon. The process by which trees consume atmospheric carbon, in the form of carbon dioxide, and transform it into carbohydrates is photosynthesis. Photosynthesis is the driving force behind all forest ecosystems, providing both energy and oxygen for the biotic community. Photosynthetic bacteria will also fix a small amount of carbon dioxide.

The carbohydrates produced by photosynthesis are incorporated into the growing plant body. The forest animals, including insects, are also hungrily waiting for these carbohydrates, especially the sugars! Sugars are energy and food for the growing bodies of the non-photosynthetic creatures.

Animals metabolize these plant sugars to produce carbon dioxide gas as a waste product every time they exhale. Plants also exhale carbon dioxide into the atmosphere, where it can again enter the plant's pores and be turned back into sugars and other carbohydrates to complete the cycle. Not all of the world's carbon is constantly in flux. Some of it stays put, by being incorporated into the plant bodies.

WHY WE STUDY ECOSYSTEMS: SERVICES

We study the forest ecosystem in order to learn how best to preserve it. One reason ecologists want to preserve it is that the forest provides us with many services. Perhaps no service is more important than helping us manage water. In fact, watershed preservation was the major impetus behind the U.S. government's

1891 decision to set aside lands for public forest reserves. This is also the reason that foresters generally identify each forest ecosystem with a particular watershed. A watershed is a sloped piece of land that sheds its water, collected from rain and snowmelt, into a distinct river system. Sometimes the slope is nearly imperceptible, but almost all landscape in the continent belongs to a watershed.

A forested watershed allows water to seep slowly into the soil and drain slowly into its collecting basin or waterway. A forested watershed may prevent a torrential rainfall from becoming a flood. These floods can erode meadows into bare, unusable rock. The dirt and debris pouring down the unforested slopes will eventually shed into running water. The water, perhaps a creek or river, will become cloudy and warmer and lose oxygen as a result. This in turn creates an inhospitable environment for many fish species, including most members of the trout family.

Flooding following deforestation of a watershed, followed by the loss of fish habitat, occurred in Panama during the spring of 2005. The magnitude of the disaster was such that the country has begun large-scale forest ecosystem protection. Unfortunately, the watersheds that are currently denuded will be nearly impossible to restore since the floods have left the sites without soil.

Although critical, erosion and flood control is not the only reason ecologists want to save forests. Forests provide the living world with a source of oxygen. The process of photosynthesis, which produces usable carbohydrates, also splits water into oxygen. Although plants can survive without oxygen because they produce more than they use, animals cannot, thus you should not be surprised that plants inhabited the planet for many hundreds of millions of years before there was sufficient oxygen to support large animals.

Forests also mitigate temperature extremes and provide windbreaks that help dampen dust storms and moderate extreme cold.

THREATS TO FORESTS

Ecologists don't just study energy flows and services provided, they are also concerned with anything that threatens an ecosystem. The two most important threats are deforestation, the ultimate transformation of the forest to meadow or asphalt, and the current warming and drying of the planet. Deforestation began in North America with the influx of large numbers of Europeans concomitant with their needs of fuel, housing material, and space. Open space was needed for houses and cities, growing crops, and raising livestock. These needs fueled the largest deforestation we have ever seen on this continent. Logging removed 70% of the old growth Douglas fir forests in Oregon and Washington between 1890 and 1989. We need to use some caution when dealing with the term *old growth* as it has many definitions. In this case, old growth was defined as any forest that had not previously been logged or burned, *by Europeans*, and was at least 300 years old. Some researchers define old growth based on the percentage of dead and down trees and snags, and/or the complexity of the forest (meaning total number of tree species of various ages). Forest reduction continues today at a much slower pace, partially due to the saturation of open space and livestock, and also because ecosystem services provided by the forest are highly valued.

Currently, the biggest threat to forests is global warming. Meteorologists expect North America to continue warming for the next 50 years, beyond which time predictions become less accurate. In the far north, melting permafrost may drown the boreal forests. Encouraged by a temperature increase of 2°–3°F in the last decade, the melting has already begun, and birch trees are already falling into newly created Alaskan swamps. Along with the warming, a drying trend threatens the Great Plains, making it virtually impossible for forests to return. We also know that warming and drying helps wildfires take a bigger bite out of forests.

What Are the Effects of Deforestation?

Deforestation, the removal of forests to make room for human uses such as agricultural and urban areas, is a common phenomenon as human population increases. Scientists have discovered some curious effects of deforestation. For example, glaciers on Mt. Kilimanjaro in Tanzania, Africa, have shrunk 80% in the last 100 years. The rate is such that one ecologist predicts their demise in the next decade. Humans and other living things depend upon the very slow melting of glaciers to provide vital drinking water, so the cause of the shrinking is of great concern. Is it global warming? Increased volcanism? Maybe, but one team of ecologists believes deforestation is playing a critical role. When the forests at the base of the mountain became croplands, the rains stopped.

Leaves transpire water back into the atmosphere, causing trees to act as rainmakers. Recall that during the great circling and recycling of water around the planet, forests take in atmospheric water and produce oxygen in the process of photosynthesis. This process is reversed during transpiration, the evaporation of water from leaves. Forests have a lot of leafy matter and are both horizontal and vertical ecosystems. They are net suppliers of water to the atmosphere. In fact, forests exhale more moisture into the atmosphere than either crop or grassland ecosystems.

Scientists are reporting similar effects of deforestation on the water bank of the Amazon basin, where less water returning to the clouds means less rain falling in the basin. Scientists have used the unique chemical properties of the water molecule to track water traveling from the forests to the Amazon River to the ocean and back again. This South American deforestation is being blamed for a reduction of rainfall in Midwestern North America.

Knowing how closely tied the forest ecosystem is to the global cycles of carbon, water, and other nutrients, this should not surprise you. Is there deforestation in your habitat? What do you think the effects might be?

Climate change is evident and data already demonstrate that the last decade was warmer. Effects of the warming are also evident. What is not evident is how climate changes will affect forests. Whether these trends will continue or be mitigated or exacerbated by other warming-induced processes we do not know. We can predict that the Earth is warming, however, we can only predict some but not all of the repercussions.

Connections

Dr. Eugene Odum created a new vision—ecosystems—the web of living things and their environment. Looking through Odum's eyes, we see critical elements—water, energy, and nutrients—cycling and recycling among a network of interrelated organisms.

Carbon, nitrogen, and water all have gaseous and solid phases and all must meet specific requirements in order to be usable to trees. All members of the forest ecosystem share these finite resources by using them, altering them, and passing them on. The dependence on these elements binds the ecosystem together. Carbon travels from the atmosphere to living things by way of photosynthesis, and back to the atmosphere by way of respiration and combustion. We will return to this topic in Chapter 8. There is a fixed amount of carbon in the world. At any given moment, all of our carbon is either cycling or in reserve. Most of the world's carbon reserve is in forests, attached to the tissues of the trees.

Ecologists study the cycling of energy, water, and nutrients partially in order to conserve ecosystems, because most biologists believe in the preservation of life forms. But also because forest ecosystems provide services: the mitigation of temperature extremes, flooding, erosion, and water loss.

We continue discussing ecosystems in the final two chapters. Next, we concentrate on the biotic factors within the ecosystem and finally, in Chapter 8, we will examine both biotic and abiotic factors as fire sweeps across a forest. Dr. Odum's vision has moved us forward but it cannot do so indefinitely. Who will be the next visionary?

7 Forest Animals

*We must protect the forests for those
who can't speak for themselves
such as the birds, animals, fish, and trees.*
— Chief Edward Moody

Forest Animals

As a backcountry ranger at Mt. Rainier National Park, I spent hundreds of days alone hiking forested mountains and valleys, and yet was never lonely. In these forests of the Pacific Northwest conifer zone, I found dozens of animal species. A typical hike to a peak on the southeast side of the mountain starts with a greeting from mountain chickadees and Oregon juncos enjoying the open canopy at the forest's indistinct edge. Under solid tree cover, in the moist forest where delicate lacy branches of yew dominate the subcanopy, I find slugs, tree frogs, leopard frogs, and the wet wallows of wapiti, the American elk. There are a few white pines here—survivors of the last century's blister rust disaster. Many of the trees are over 300 years old and in their bountiful shade I often hear or see pileated woodpeckers. Climbing again into the drier south-facing slopes, I try to grab the bright blue tail of a juvenile western skink but it slithers under a downed pine tree. My commotion has disturbed a pine squirrel busy burying a huge cache of Douglas fir cones into his corner of the forest. As I continue climbing, red-tailed hawks, almost always visible through large areas of open canopy, are screaming. One day a hawk swooped right in front of me to pick up a robin for its lunch. Continuing through the avalanche chutes that decorate the forest in long fingers of blueberries, I almost always see black bears, as many as seven in a single day. At the summit, where the flag trees wave, mountain goats sit among pockets of them. A pine marten running along a nurse log misses the squirrel it was chasing and heads up into the branches of a spruce where he makes his home. Next to the marten's home, in a dead snag, I once watched a three-toed woodpecker family with little yellow-capped heads, all working in unison on their way up the tree.

How does the forest fit such a great variety of animals? The main reason is that the forest is highly variable. This forest is not a tree farm; it is a relatively free association of wild organisms. Every nook and cranny seems to house a separate species. The ecological term for "nook and cranny" is **niche**. Each niche is located within a specific habitat.

Habitat describes the physical characteristics of the place where the animal lives. This includes the location, climate, and the plant community. Animals have habitats that they prefer and in which they prosper and increase, and marginal habitats in which they may exist but only in dwindling numbers. On a marginal habitat, animals may be in the process of becoming extinct. Each species has habitat requirements. Sometimes they overlap, and sometimes they conflict. For example, grizzly bears do not require a forested habitat, but black bears do. Fires or deforestation may not directly decrease the grizzly's survival, but it will decrease the number of black bears (Figure 7.1).

Within the habitat, an animal's niche describes both its particular space and its occupation. Since animals spend a great deal of their lives eating, we usually define their occupation according to what and when they eat. For example, those that eat insects are insectivores and plant eaters are **herbivores**. Animals that feed early and late in the day are crepuscular and those that feed in the middle of the day are diurnal. Ecologists choose the word *niche* to describe this phenomenon because the literal meaning, "a spot in the wall," closely approximates the way that animals divide the habitat to make use of every habitable crack in the forest house. Chickadees, flickers, owls, and goshawks can all share the same spruce-fir forest because the chickadees eat tree insects, the flickers eat ground ants, the owl eats mice, and the goshawk eats the chickadees, flickers, and owls.

BIODIVERSITY

The greater the number of different species, the greater the biodiversity. The more species in a habitat will result in greater biodiversity for that habitat. The importance of this concept belies (or hides) its slipperiness. Biodiversity is a measure lacking a unit. If you want to know the average temperature

Figure 7.1 The American black bear is a forest obligate. He is completely dependent on the forest for his livelihood.

of a forest, you will find a number that will be expressed as a unit. Degrees Fahrenheit is a unit, as are centimeters, inches, kilograms, etc. In the absence of units, biodiversity is usually expressed as the number of species present. Forests have more biodiversity than tree farms, and we know that, in general, older forests and forests near the tropics have more biodiversity than colder forests and younger forests.

A generally accepted ecological principal is that an ecosystem with high biodiversity, in other words species rich, is healthier than one that is species poor. Why do you suppose this is? In general, unless you're talking about something bad, like chicken pox, the more you have, the better you are. Having a lot of species buffers us against tragedy. For example, if the avian flu wipes out all the wood ducks and geese, that would be tragic, but at least if we have many other similar species that survived, the epidemic would be less tragic. Also, consider events such as earthquakes, volcanoes, avalanches, and hurricanes, all of which can wipe out small populations—so the more species there are, the greater the degree of buffering from environmental disasters.

Another reason high biodiversity is desirable is to keep all the jobs in the system active, all the niches filled, so to speak. Suppose a species, such as the rattlesnake, has a job that entails eating field mice that hide under woody shrubs during the day. If we wipe out rattlesnakes, field mice could become overpopulated. Leaving as many species as possible means there is likely to be someone around when a job needs doing. Unfortunately, we can't always predict which jobs need doing, so keeping as many species as possible makes sense. As Aldo Leopold, the "Father of wildlife management," warns in the classic *Sand County Almanac,* the first rule for ecosystem management is "to save all the parts."

Forests support animal biodiversity by providing food and shelter. A surprisingly large number of animals depend upon the forest in varying degrees (Figure 7.2). Animals that cannot survive without the forest are **obligate forest dwellers**, while those that enjoy forests, but can survive without them, are **facultative** dependents. Dependent mammals are obliged by genetics and physiology to reside within the forest and their existence is completely tied to the forest. For example, practical extinction visited both the ivory-billed woodpecker and the passenger pigeon as a direct result of the massive logging of their forest homes. Both

Figure 7.2 This mountain sheep is a facultative dweller in the forest. He can survive without forest lands, but on a hot summer day, he'll take advantage of the shade when possible.

these species were dependent upon mature forests and could not survive in tree farm replacements.

Animals that depend upon forest products directly for food are **primary consumers**. Insects, birds, mammals, and reptiles all consume the crops of the forest, either the nuts, fruits, and seeds, collectively called **mast**, or the leaves and twigs of the forest trees. Oak acorns are by far the most important mast crop for wildlife throughout North America. Herbivores, animals that consume young woody material, are primary consumers. Animals that eat the primary consumers are **secondary consumers**. Snakes, hawks, and mountain lions are secondary consumers.

BIRDS

Among animals that depend upon the forest, none are more dependent than birds. Half of all North American birds are forest obligates and fill a variety of niches. There are cavity-nesting birds, some of which depend upon the holes left in a tree by shed branches, while others excavate their own cavities. Still others repossess the cavities of small mammals. Small cavity-nesters eat insects and larva. Midsized birds are often woodpeckers, and larger cavity-nesters such as owls eat other birds and mammals. In order to fill all these niches, there must be some standing dead trees, and there must be some very large diameter trees, dead or alive. The spotted owl raised a lot of concern in the Pacific Northeast because of its particular habitat requirements. This owl needs to burrow right into trees, but it's a large bird, and cannot fit inside small trees. The only way to get trees to live to be very big is to avoid cutting them down while they are small.

Some very large birds such as raptors (hunting birds) inhabit our forests. Accipiters (forest hawks) are so large they rarely live inside trees, but depend upon external nests that need to sit on very large branches. Not only do forest hawks need large branches to support the weight of their nests, but also branches that are far apart so they can perch upright without bumping their heads. Trees with branches close together are not suitable, nor are trees with strongly inclined or declined branches. In fact, these birds have very narrow habitat requirements. They prefer members of the pine family that have large diameter upper branches that tend toward horizontal, or very flat growth, and often extend out longer than the branches below them.

Insect-feeding birds enjoy older, wilder forests that may contain diseased trees. Woodpeckers thrive in areas with ample dead or infected trees. This is one reason that ecologists may recommend against salvage harvesting after a fire. The fire-killed trees attract insects that in turn attract woodpeckers.

Birds are one of the main consumers of forest nuts. Acorns and pine nuts are especially desirable and many species of birds are dependent upon forest trees for their survival for this reason alone. The forest in turn receives benefits from the birds that spread the tree seeds far distances. Whitebark and limber pines produce fat, tasty seeds, revered by most animals, humans, bears, squirrels, and birds. When the Clark's nutcracker is lucky enough to get hold of the seeds, she will secret them away in a stash pile out of the forest. If she doesn't eat all the seeds, some may germinate and extend the range of the forest. This now classic tale about the nutcracker's forgotten seed stash explains the existence of many whitebark and limber pines in the North American high country.

MAMMALS

Many mammals are forest obligates; others merely rely on it to shelter them from harsh weather or feared enemies, or perhaps provide a source of prey. Mammals cannot flee harsh weather as easily as birds, so many need the forest for winter survival, especially in the northern conifer and northern hardwoods

Figure 7.3 Like many other non-hibernating mammals in the cold regions, this snowshoe hare depends upon trees to hold in the heat; without the forest for shelter, he might not survive the winter.

forest. These forest habitats help confine heat close to the ground and prevent non-hibernating mammals from freezing to death. Weasels, rabbits, elk, caribou, deer, and wolverine are some of the animals that snuggle under the forest canopy for warmth in the northern latitudes (Figure 7.3).

Like birds, many mammals have distinct habitat requirements. Lynx are very particular about forests with thick underbrush. Caribou depend upon ancient forests that provide an abundance of their favorite food, lichen. Moose eat from young hardwood forests, but need softwood forests for protection from wolves.

HERBIVORY

Herbivores are animals that eat parts of plants. Animals that eat woody parts are browsing herbivores, and grass eaters are grazing herbivores. The herbivores with the most influence on forests are insects. Insects tend to be specialized herbivores, focusing on specific species of trees, while mammals tend to be generalists,

Forests on the Receiving End of Herbivory

Knowing that insect herbivores are primary consumers, we often accuse them of munching away on vital forest foliage. But the general wisdom of ecology suggests that the forest is web of resource sharing characterized by *mutual* benefits. Most of the animal relationships within the forest community are obscure, so ecologists continue to examine components of the ecosystem asking, *"What role does this population play?"* Louie H. Yang, a graduate student at the University of California, Davis, recently discovered a new role for those pesky, noisy, ugly cicadas. They feed the forest.

Yang's research, recorded in the journal *Science,* began as the scientific process always does, with observations. He observed that growth spurts in forest trees occur during those rare years when cicadas emerge. During the years 2001–2004, Yang and his colleagues dumped millions of cicada carcasses in an experimental forest.* They then recorded increases in soil bacteria, fungi, and nitrogen, which they were able to trace to the decomposing bug bodies. Ecological effects that spike periodically are but both prefer young leaves, shoots, and buds, and neither causes much damage at **endemic** levels. The endemic level is the level native to an area. Insect eating habits are a normal function of the ecosystem and the insects repay the favor by pollinating trees. Although the gymnosperms are entirely wind pollinated, 70% of forest tree *species* (not trees) in North America depend upon animal pollinators, mostly insects.

When herbivory exceeds endemic levels, we have an epidemic or a breakout. Some insects rarely breakout, others do so regularly. Eastern and western varieties of spruce budworm, gypsy moth, and mountain pine beetle are among the most common breakout herbivores in North America. Insects are specialized, preferring to dine on just a single species, and sometimes they

called pulses. Cicadas, it seems, cause a nitrogen pulse in the forest. Knowing that nitrogen is an important resource for the forest and that its incorporation into the soil is rare, you certainly appreciate how important this pulse is for forest productivity. This story reinforces Dr. Odum's ideas: the forest is an interacting community of organisms relying on each other. Many of the ways that the plants and animals in the forest rely on each other are obscure, but that's what makes forest ecology such an exciting field.

This story illustrates three basic niches: production, consumption, and decomposition. The forest plants produce carbohydrates, the cicadas consume the plants and die, and the fungi decompose the cicadas and release the nitrogen from their bodily proteins back into the soil. From there, the nitrogen is consumed by the plant roots to begin the cycle all over again.

———

*See the sidebar in Chapter 8 for a description of experimental forests.

are even restricted to a particular population of a species. Insects are also selective regarding age and size of the trees upon which they feed and lay eggs. This is another reason that ecologists champion biodiversity: the greater the variety, the more likely it is that some trees will survive an epidemic.

Consider the rampantly aggressive spruce budworm. In some western forests, logging practices have selectively removed the trees with the highest monetary value—Ponderosa and Larch—two species that are also budworm resistant. Remaining behind are the susceptible firs, and the insects are having a holiday in forests filled with their favorite food. Dead branches from the infected firs may increase the possibility of fire. If fires become more frequent, firs may succeed to pines and start the cycle all over again. So, what exactly are the ultimate effects of an epidemic? There are no ultimate effects—the ecosystem keeps moving in complex ways.

Even epidemics, although they cause large areas of defoliation (removal of leafy parts), are rarely fatal. Like any disease, they cause the infected party to weaken and grow more slowly. Although this is not a helpful trait on a tree farm, in a forest patches of sick trees are normal. Mountain pine beetle is a notable exception, which is almost always fatal to the host if the invading beetle is carrying spores from bluestain fungus.

Connections

Within the forest ecosystem, complex webs describe the relationships between the forest and the animals that either visit or live entirely within. Insects, birds, and mammals all take from and give back to the forest. Animals and forests influence each other in still unknown ways. Sleuthing out these relationships is a fun, challenging, and never-ending task for ecologists. Next time you visit a forest, bring a notepad and try to work out the complex web. Who is eating whom? Who is providing the energy for the system? What other services are individual species needing, and what services are they providing?

In our next chapter, we will put together what we have learned about trees, forests, and forest ecology and apply this to fire management.

*. . . When a giant falls, leaving a little space . . .
then there's a race—between the trees on either side,
who want to spread out, and the seedlings below,
who race to grow up.*

— Terry Pratchett

Fire in the Forest

Three thousand years ago in the Pacific Northwest, people sit around a campfire making plans for the fire season. Descendants of the Paleo-Indians are wearing clothes they have fashioned from animals that were trapped, killed, skinned, reworked, and then sewn with tools. The descendants make needles, baskets, pottery, jewelry, and houses. Although they are competent tool-makers, fire is their most important tool. May is a wet and windy month, so they seek the shelter of the Douglas fir forests and sit on large logs under the spreading canopy of trees with bark so thick it is almost fire resistant. The undergrowth is sparse and park-like; the grasses are coming in fast and green. They are sitting in an area they burned in previous years. Now they are discussing doing more burns for other parts of the tribe's territory.

The question is difficult. As with all forestry issues, human values will be involved, as well as facts that are yet unknown and possibly never will be known. Most of the tribe enjoys the way the burned forest encourages the movement of men and game, and they appreciate the improved quality of forage. Their neighbors to the east, the Plains peoples, have long known that burning the thatch and the shrubs off the prairies allows grasses to get sunlight and water, producing improved forage for the buffalo. Still, there are voices of concern. An out-of-control fire is a serious threat; suppression is technologically demanding and is not an option. Although not common, the elders of the tribe recall stories of Plains people burned when fires were out of control. They know about buffalo dying in fast-moving prairie firestorms. One advantage to the lifestyle of the people 3,000 years ago is that the lodges, forerunners of today's teepees, could be packed up and moved if necessary, but that would only be practical for controlled fires. A surprise fire would give them less time to pack up and move.

There is no doubt that these discussions actually occurred. While we don't know the outcome, it appears that Indians did set many fires in the Pacific Northwest thousands of years ago.

Ecologists believe that the Douglas fir strands of Oregon, Washington, and Northern California are the direct result of prehistoric human activity. It's possible that Indians set fires intentionally, as discussed above, and also unintentionally. Because millions of people relied solely on fire for heat and cooking, we can't rule out accidental fires. The most common source of fire was probably lightning strikes that aboriginal people did not suppress, either by choice or by chance.

Today, we face similar issues in forest fire management. Sometimes we act upon choice, and other times upon chance. Also, we must still combine facts with values when learning about forest fires. We'll start this chapter with the chemical, physical, and biological facts about fire in the forests.

WHAT IS FIRE?

Fire is a rapidly occurring chemical reaction, essentially the burning of sugar in the presence of oxygen. We represent chemical reactions with equations showing inputs on the left side and outputs on the right side of the equal sign. Here is the forest fire equation:

$$O_2 + \text{Carbohydrate} + \text{source of heat} = H_2O + CO_2 + \text{heat and light}$$

O_2 is the symbol for oxygen, H_2O for water, and CO_2 for carbon dioxide

Oxygen is a necessary element for fire; this is why we stop fires by smothering them. Aerially applied chemical retardants work by preventing oxygen from reaching the fire. Fire also needs fuel, which is anything that burns, but in the forest these are primarily organic molecules from living or dead plants. A secondary source of fuel is organic matter from animals, fungi, or bacteria. Even with fuel and oxygen, the fire reaction must usually be primed, or given an initial impetus or jolt, with heat.

The fire reaction, combustion, releases carbon dioxide, heat and light, and water. Many people are surprised that fire releases water. Fire actually plays a significant role in the cycling of water through the atmosphere. Next time you are lucky enough to witness a huge firestorm, note what appears to be a cumulus cloud above the column of flame and smoke. That cloud is a result of the vast quantity of water released during the combustion of organic material produced by photosynthesis. Can you see the role that fire plays in the water cycle? Plants uptake groundwater, fire releases the water from the plants into the atmosphere, and within about 12 days all the water in the clouds will fall back to the Earth.

Experimental Forests

Our collective knowledge about North American forests often comes from research occurring on the experimental forests managed by the U.S. Forest Service (USFS) and the Canadian Forest Service. Most of the experimental forests are located on public land. That's not too surprising in Canada, where all but 6% of the forests are under public ownership. The purpose of an experimental forest is to provide controlled areas for long-term ecological research. Learning about forest ecosystems would be nearly impossible without experimental forests because controls are necessary to achieve the best level of understanding. To control an experiment, scientists perform an activity called a *treatment* in one designated area, and leave an identical area without treatment. In the case of fire studies, the treatment would usually be fire.

One of the most famous stations, established in 1955, is the Hubbard Brook Experimental Forest in New Hampshire's White Mountains. Soon after its establishment, Hubbard Brook initiated a forest ecosystem study (HBES) to investigate the mechanisms and pathways of water and nutrient cycling. The experiments generally involved some kind of anthropogenic disturbance. These are human initiated disturbances, for

Where does the fire get the oxygen and fuel? Can you pick out the reaction that is the opposite of fire? There is one common reaction that takes the products of fire, water, and carbon dioxide and turns them into the necessary reactants for fire: oxygen and fuel. For example:

$$CO_2 + H_2O + sun = sugar + O_2$$

The chemical equation illustrates photosynthesis. Plants are busy working all day to build up the sugars and oxygen that fires rapidly dispose of. Fire and photosynthesis are opposite

example, air and water pollution, logging, and some types of wildfire. By contrast, avalanches and floods are natural disturbances and therefore not anthropogenic.

There are 11 experimental forests in the southeastern U.S. Most exist in order to support studies about the repair and regeneration of heavily impacted forest ecosystems. The Calhoun Experimental Forest in South Carolina and Alabama's Escambia longleaf pine forests both sponsor studies on short-term fire response and long-term ecosystem level effects of fire.

Researchers working in the oak-pine zone of the Little Tallahatchie Experimental Forest in Alabama have found that beech is negatively affected by fire, and that forest tree communities do not vary with the changing frequency of experimental fires. Surprisingly, in the short run, they have been unable to increase the fire tolerant oaks and shortleaf pine by burning.

Experimental forests will no doubt continue to play a key role in fire research and in ecosystem level research of the future. If you are considering a career in forest ecology, don't overlook the limitless opportunities afforded by forest experiment stations.

reactions, but can you think of another reaction that is the same as fire? Fire is a chemical reaction identical to animal metabolism, the process by which all animals obtain energy. As animals, we are, of course, close competitors with fire. We consume the same products and expel the same waste. Combustion and metabolism are identical. We can kill a fire the same way we kill any living thing: deprive it of oxygen. We depend on food and fire depends on fuel—two names for nearly identical needs.

WHAT IS FUEL?

Although fuel is anything that burns, the bulk of it comes from the products of photosynthesis—organic carbon molecules, sugars, and cellulose found living in dead forest plants.

We categorize fuel according to its position in the forest: horizontal, vertical, or canopy. Horizontal fuels lie along the forest floor, generally composed of dead trees and limbs that carry the fire forward and allow it to move outward along the ground. Although they are horizontal and parallel to the forest floor, these fuels may pile up many feet high. Vertical fuels are called **ladder fuels** because they allow the fire to climb up into treetops as though they were walking up a ladder. Ladder fuels may consist of small trees, shrubs, or branches on a tall tree. Many species of pine shed their lower branches as they grow to rid themselves of fire ladder. Sometimes the plan backfires, however. A fir or a juniper, both of which are highly flammable, may grow nuzzled around a pine tree, where the shed branches have left a large opening. This decreases the natural fire resistance of the pine. Since the firs and juniper are likely to die in any fire, they might as well take the pine out with them.

The typical forest fire crawls along the ground, occasionally torching a particularly flammable tree. The rare fires that do reach the treetops and burn across the canopy fuels are called crown fires (Figure 8.1).

Figure 8.1 The fire that swept through here moved through the crowns of the trees, burning off most foliage and branches. Crown fires are more common where trees are close together and winds are strong.

Fuel is also categorized into four size classes: one-, ten-, 100-, and 1,000-hour fuels. Although most scientific measurements use the metric system, we always measure fuel size in the English system. A one-hour fuel is a piece of wood, usually a twig, less than one-quarter inch in diameter. A ten-hour fuel is a small branch between one-quarter and one-inch diameter. Trunks from small trees or large branches between one and three inches diameter are 100-hour fuels. Anything with a diameter greater than three inches is a 1,000-hour fuel. We use these measurements to estimate how long it will take for fuel to become dry. In the spring, at the beginning of the fire season, the fuels are very wet and soaked with snow or spring rain. As the air becomes drier, so does the fuel. A one-hour fuel takes about an hour to equilibrate (become equivalent) to the ambient (surrounding air) relative humidity. A 1,000-hour fuel, usually consisting of trees, takes 1,000 hours. How many days is that? The measurements also tell us how long it will take for the fuels to become safely wet again after the rains begin in the fall. After two days of rain, many people wonder why the forest service is still so worried about fires. This is because if the 1,000-hour fuels were desiccated, it will take 1,000 hours (that's much more than two days) to dampen down below the fire danger.

Fine fuels are the tiniest grasses and needles that react almost immediately to changes in the ambient relative humidity. Fires generally cannot start without an available supply of dry fine fuels. Think about throwing a match into a forest with nothing but trees and soil. You wouldn't expect that match to start a fire. Throwing a match is analogous to the sparks, called firebrands, which are thrown off by a tree that has been hit by lightning. The lightning is likely to take down that single tree and a few others whose branches are close enough to engulf in flame, but how can the strike cause a wildfire? If firebrands from the burning tree do not land on anything small enough and dry enough (kindling, in other words) to combust, then the fire will soon die. The small fuels are generally annuals, those plants that are produced every spring and die in the fall. This is why spring rain is so critical, and often paradoxical. Rain promotes plant growth. Seeds in the soil bank have been waiting for warm water in order to germinate. In the case of annual plants, or fine fuels, what greens up also browns down. In the late summer, all the new growth stimulated by a rainy spring will become cured (dried) fine fuel, ready to ignite at the touch of a firebrand.

Consider the opposite scenario: spring drought. Very little new growth means the forest floor and neighboring meadows are mostly dirt, and dirt doesn't burn. It should not surprise you that one of the worst fire years in the west's recent history was 1988—one of wettest springs on record.

FIRE IN THE ECOSYSTEM

Fire occurs in all forest ecosystems and is neither good nor bad. Neither is it neutral. The effects of fire help some members of the ecosystem and harm others. The degree to which organisms benefit or suffer in a fire is related to the characteristics of the individual fire and the characteristics of the organism.

Important characteristics of a forest fire are the speed at which it travels, the heat at which it burns, and the height of the flames. Together with the frequency with which fire occurs, these characteristics are called the **fire regime**.

Tree species that can withstand fire are fire tolerant (Figure 8.2). Since not all organisms are fire tolerant, those that are benefit by gaining a competitive advantage over those that are not. In the absence of fire, fire-tolerant species may surrender some territory. Hardwood forests, preferring wetter and lower areas than evergreens, experience low-intensity fires and do not possess many fire-tolerant attributes. Two notable exceptions are oak and aspen. This should not surprise you, since both these genera grow among pines in dry fire-prone evergreen forests. After a fire, aspen regenerates rapidly using underground suckers. By removing decadent trees and encouraging new growth, fires are often helpful to aspen. Oak, the most common hardwood in dry, hot forests, develop a thick bark and increase their fire resistance as they age. In very hot fires that destroy all above ground portions, old oaks may resprout from underground trunks.

Figure 8.2 Fires generally burn along the ground, leaving the forest charred or scorched. Sometimes fires will burn through the forest canopy killing trees but leaving blackened branches and cones visible. Catastrophic fire, an uncommon regime, carved these trees into totem poles.

Gymnosperms have evolved in many ways to tolerate fire, including their means of reproduction, general shape, bark quality, and growth patterns. After a fire, it is not unusual to find that a majority of seeds on the ground are spruce or pine. Spruces sequester their cones high on the tree so that most fires, being ground hugging, will not be able to reach the cones. Some pines have serotinous cones, meaning that they can withstand fire by virtue of a thick resin sealant. Serotiny is a genetic trait characteristic of species or populations.

Another adaptation to fire is self-pruning, the act of shedding lower branches that are in harm's way when ground fires burn. Self-pruning happens when branches die and are attacked by fungi. They subsequently drop off due to wind, animals, or gravity. Pruning occurs more rapidly in warm, wet climates because that is where fungi thrive. The only tree species in North American forests that **self-prune** are longleaf, slash, and redpine.

Douglas fir and some of the pine species have bark too thick for most fires to penetrate. Spruce and some other pine species have papery bark, which offers little protection, while firs are downright flammable with thin bark that is covered with pitch blisters. The pitch is highly flammable. Firs are ill-adapted to fire for another reason as well: their branches sweep along the ground and allow fires to climb the ladder of their limbs right up to the crown. Spruce has a similar conformation but fortunately tends to inhabit areas that don't burn often.

FOREST FIRE TODAY

Not much has changed in several thousand years. Time cannot rewrite the basic chemical and physical equations of fire. We have better means of fire suppression, but those methods still fail, and when they do, we have the same fire effects that our ancestors experienced. Prescription fires, ignited by foresters, are as common today as they were thousands of years ago.

One reason foresters set fires today is to keep trees from growing into meadows. The Nature Conservancy has set fires in the Black Hills to prevent "ponderosa pine encroachment," and the National Park Service sets fires in the Tetons to prevent "Douglas fir encroachment."

One thing that has changed is our culture's mobility. North American people no longer pick up their teepees and move with the fire season. And wood has become easy, as opposed to nearly impossible, to harvest. The demand for wood has increased and many folks are not anxious to see a profitable resource go up in smoke. This has led to an increased call for fire suppression.

Along with that desire, we have increased our ability to suppress fires by adding chainsaws, chemical retardants, helicopters, and wildland fire engines to our arsenal. We use satellites to track lightning strikes, and fixed wings to fly the strikes and look for smoke. An industry, a culture, and an economy have grown up around fire suppression in the same way that they have around logging. Many communities have come to depend upon the income generated by fire suppression activities.

The whims of culture are more transient than fire facts, but no less important in the study of forests. We continue to follow the crooked creek of culture as it changes suddenly, unpredictably, and always too rapidly. But we must never lose sight of the steadfast, slower moving river of science. There is still so much room, so many questions, and so many phenomena waiting for your observation.

Conclusion

As guardians of the forest planet, we have inherited the legacy of the ancient giant evergreens struggling to maintain their hold on this rapidly warming Earth. We watch the young, aggressive, wild angiosperms travel in every direction, but perhaps never prepared for the desires that man would have upon their wood.

Demanding of water, but intolerant of swamps, where will these babes of the woods be in 100 years? The information we gather and the directions we choose will determine the answers. When we answer for the forest, we answer for all the nonliving things—water, carbon, and nitrogen—and all the living things—animals, fungi, insects, and flowers. We also answer for ourselves, guardians of the universe's only Forest Planet.

Glossary

Agriculture The farming of crops and livestock.

Angiosperm A plant whose reproductive parts are a flower, and whose seeds are contained in an ovary.

Annual ring A layer of wood formed during a single year.

Apical bud The undeveloped plant shoot at the tip of a stem.

Apical meristem Growing tissue at the tip of a root or stem.

Biomass The total dry weight of all living things in a given area.

Boreal A northern region, also the forests of the northern latitudes.

Browse To consume woody parts of plants.

Cambium A cylindrical layer of growing tissue around the stems and roots that will give rise to bark and woody plant vasculature.

Canopy The interlaced crowns of trees.

Carpel The part of the flower that encloses one or more ovules. The mature ovule will become a seed.

Climax community The assemblage of tree species that represent the end of succession because they are stable (in the absence of disturbance) and self-perpetuating.

Community A group of interacting species living in a particular area or ecosystem.

Conifer A tree that bears its seeds in a cone.

Coniferophyta The group of plants that bear their seeds in a cone.

Cotyledon An embryonic leaf inside a seed.

Deciduous Dropping leaves once a year.

Decurrent Having a rounded shape.

Dicot An angiosperm that has two embryonic leaves inside its seed.

Disturbance Any relatively discrete event in space and time that disrupts an ecosystem, community, or population structure and changes resources, substrate, or the physical environment.

Dormancy A period in which the plant's growth is halted and can only be restarted upon certain environmental cues.

Duff A semi-consolidated layer of decomposing organic litter on the forest floor.

Ecology The study of the interrelationships among living things and between living things and their physical environment.

Endemic Native to an area. The low population level that occurs naturally.

Excurrent The tree shape normally associated with spruce and many other conifers; characterized by one main undivided trunk.

Facultative forest dweller An animal living in the forest by choice but not obligated by its genetic makeup or physiological requirements to do so.

Fascicles Bundles of needles attached to a pine tree.

Fen An inland marsh.

Fire regime The historical pattern and description of natural fire in an area, including its severity, speed, and temporal characteristics.

Forbs Flowering plants that are not woody and are not grasses.

Fruit A product of the angiosperm flower consisting of the mature ovary and seeds.

Germination The beginning of growth, or the resumption of growth following dormancy, by a plant.

Gymnosperm A member of the plant family whose seeds are not enclosed in an ovary (and therefore does not produce fruit).

Habitat A description of the place where a living thing dwells or is usually found.

Hardwood A common term for the wood of an angiosperm tree.

Herbivores Animals that consume living plants.

Hypothesis A testable explanation or a proposal created following observations.

Imperfect flower The reproductive structure of an angiosperm that is missing either pistils or stamen.

Ladder fuels Combustible material that is continuous from the ground up into the crown of a tree.

Glossary

Lateral buds Buds found along the length of the twig (not at the tip); they occur where the previous year's leaves were attached.

Lateral meristem Growing cells that produce secondary plant tissue: the vascular cambium and the bark. The common use of the word *cambium* has the same definition.

Life cycle The entire sequence of growth phases of an organism, beginning with the fertilized egg and ending at maturity.

Litter Debris from plant bodies (leaves, twigs, needles) accumulating on the forest floor that has not undergone any noticeable decomposition and is loose and unconsolidated.

Magnoliophyta Formal term for angiosperms; the division within the plant kingdom that includes all angiosperms. Also called Anthophyta.

Mast Edible nuts and seeds from trees.

Megasporangia In gymnosperms, the structure that holds the ovules. Commonly called a "pinecone."

Microsporangia In gymnosperms, the structure that holds the pollen; pollen cone.

Monoecious A plant bearing both egg and pollen on the same tree.

Niche The role or job of a living thing in its habitat, and its relationships with other living and nonliving things in its environment.

Obligate forest dweller An animal whose genetic makeup and/or physiology requires that it live in a forest in order to survive.

Paleo-Indians The name modern Americans have given to the first people to enter America from Beringia. We do not know what the people called themselves.

Perfect flower The reproductive structure of an angiosperm that includes both pistils and stamen.

Permafrost Permanently frozen land.

Pistil The part of the flower that consists of ovaries, and typically a stigma and style (the structures that receive the pollen).

Plant biogeography The study of the distribution of plants.

Primary consumers Animals that eat parts of the forest plants.

Primary growth Increase in length resulting from the apical meristems.

Primary succession Change in community composition beginning where there was no prior vegetation.

Samara A dry fruit containing one or two seeds and wings which is characteristic of, but not limited to, the maples.

Scientific method An organized way of learning that begins with making observations, generally followed by data collection, hypothesis formulation, and hypothesis testing.

Secondary consumers Animals that eat the animals that eat the forest plants.

Secondary growth The production of bark and vascular cambium in woody plants. Non-woody plants do not experience secondary growth.

Secondary succession Change in community composition beginning where there was already an established plant community.

Seed A fertilized ovule. Ovules are fertilized with pollen.

Self-prune The process by which growing trees continuously shed their lowest branches.

Seral stage Any transitory stage of development in a forest community.

Serotinous A megasporangia ("pinecone") that remains closed for many years after the seeds have matured. Generally requires high temperature in order to open.

Softwood A common term for any gymnosperm tree. The wood of a gymnosperm.

Soil seed bank Ungerminated fertilized ovules stored in the ground.

Spore A reproductive cell that does not need to be fertilized in order to produce a new being. Plants do not reproduce with spores.

Stakeholders People who have communicated an interest (monetary, social, spiritual, or otherwise) in the management of the forest.

Stamen The part of the flower including the pollen and any pollen-bearing structures.

Glossary

Stoma Openings in leaves and green stems through which gasses may enter and exit the plant.

Succession Change in plant community composition over time.

Taiga The northern coniferous forest, also called the boreal forest.

Temperate zone The area that straddles the equator, extending south to the Tropic of Capricorn and north to the Tropic of Cancer.

Transpiration The loss of water through the stoma.

Tundra A treeless area generally north of the Arctic Circle.

Virgin forest A tree-dominated ecosystem that has not been logged or burned by the Europeans.

Bonnicksen, Thomas M. *America's Ancient Forests: From the Ice Age to the Age of Discovery.* New York: John Wiley & Sons, 2000.

Hopkins, William G. and Norman P.A. Hüner. *Introduction to Plant Physiology,* Third Edition. New York: John Wiley & Sons, 2002.

Perry, Davis A. *Forest Ecosystems.* Baltimore, MD: Johns Hopkins University Press, 1994.

Pielou, E. C. *After the Ice Age.* Chicago: University of Chicago Press, 1991.

Whelan, Robert J. *The Ecology of Fire.* Cambridge: Cambridge University Press, 1995.

Young, Raymond A. and Ronald Giese. *Introduction to Forest Science,* Second Edition. New York: John Wiley & Sons, 1990.

Further Reading

Durrell, G. *A Practical Guide for the Amateur Naturalist.* London: Alfred A. Knopf, 1982.

Erickson, J. *A History of Life on Earth: Understanding Our Planet's Past.* New York: Facts on File, 1995.

Galston, A. W. *Life Processes of Plants.* New York: Scientific American Library, 1994.

Goldsworthy, A. "Why Trees are Green." *New Scientist* (December 1987).

Websites

Center for International Forestry Research
http://www.cifor.cgiar.org/

Forest Conservation Portal
http://forests.org/

Native Forest Network
http://www.nativeforest.org/

Pennsylvania Department of Conservation & Natural Resources
http://www.dcnr.state.pa.us/forestry/

Society of American Foresters
http://www.safnet.org/index.cfm

The Rainforest Foundation
http://www.rainforestfoundationuk.org/s-index

Washington Community Forestry
http://www.dnr.wa.gov/wcfc/index.html

World Resources Institute
http://www.wri.org/

Index

Index

Index

page:

11: © Photo Library International/ CORBIS

21: © Andrew Brown; Ecoscene/ CORBIS

23: Courtesy of Catherine Raven

25a: © Biodisc/Visuals Unlimited

25b: © David Sieren/Visuals Unlimited

27: Courtesy of Catherine Raven

31: Courtesy of Catherine Raven

36: Courtesy of Catherine Raven

40: Gerald & Buff Corsi/Visuals Unlimited

46: © Tim McGuire/CORBIS

48a: © James Randklev/CORBIS

48b: © Hans Strand/CORBIS

48c: © Owaki-Kulla/CORBIS

49: © HFS Imaging

54: Courtesy of Catherine Raven

63: Associated Press, DELUTH NEWS-TRIBUNE

65: © Ned Therrien/Visuals Unlimited

73: © Time Life Pictures/Getty Images

77: © HFS Imaging

84-85: Courtesy of Catherine Raven

88: Courtesy of Catherine Raven

90: Courtesy of Catherine Raven

93: Courtesy of Catherine Raven

98-99: © Momatiuk-Eastcott/CORBIS

105: © Tom Bean/CORBIS

108: Courtesy of Catherine Raven

Cover: © Corel Royalty Free Photograph

About the Author

Dr. Catherine Raven served the National Park Service for 13 seasons. Much of the commentary in this book comes from her work as a backcountry ranger at Mt. Rainier National Park, and a fire biologist at Voyageurs National Park. Her undergraduate degrees in zoology and botany are from the University of Montana, where she graduated with the President's Award in the biological sciences division. Her Ph.D. (Biology) from Montana State University earned her nomination into Sigma Xi, the honors society for scientists.

Currently an instructor at Florida Community College, Raven also spends about 10 weeks each summer teaching field classes in natural history. She designed Internet courses for college students at the University of Montana-Butte in water resource management, fire ecology, and animal conservation. She has designed and teaches classes for high school students in forest ecology, fire ecology, and animal conservation for Abaetern Academy in Bozeman, Montana.

In 2005, she published two essays on natural history in the *Journal of American Mensa.*